New Accents

General Editor: TERENCE HAWKES

LANGUAGE AND STYLE

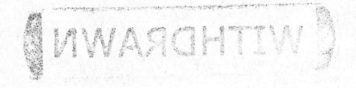

E. L. EPSTEIN

LANGUAGE AND STYLE

METHUEN & CO LTD

First published 1978 by Methuen & Co Ltd,
11 New Fetter Lane, London EC4P 4EE

© 1978 E. L. Epstein

Printed in Great Britain by
Richard Clay (The Chaucer Press) Ltd
Bungay, Suffolk

ISBN 0 416 83270 9 (hardbound)
ISBN 0 416 83280 6 (paperback)

For Tegwen

CONTENTS

GENERAL EDITOR'S PREFACE

I T is easy to see that we are living in a time of rapid and radical social change. It is much less easy to grasp the fact that such change will inevitably affect the nature of those academic disciplines that both reflect our society and help to shape it.

Yet this is nowhere more apparent than in the central field of what may, in general terms, be called literary studies. Here, among large numbers of students at all levels of education, the erosion of the assumptions and presuppositions that support the literary disciplines in their conventional form has proved fundamental. Modes and categories inherited from the past no longer seem to fit the reality experienced by a new generation.

New Accents is intended as a positive response to the initiative offered by such a situation. Each volume in the series will seek to encourage rather than resist the process of change, to stretch rather than reinforce the boundaries that currently define literature and its academic study.

Some important areas of interest will obviously be those in which an initial impetus seems to come from linguistics.

As its title suggests, one aspect of *New Accents* will be firmly located in contemporary approaches to language, and a central concern of the series will be to examine the extent to which relevant branches of linguistic studies can illuminate specific literary areas. The volumes with this particular interest will nevertheless presume no prior technical knowledge on the part of their readers, and will aim to expound the linguistics appropriate to the matter in hand, rather than to embark on general theoretical matters.

Modern linguistics has also provided a basis for the study of the totality of human communication, and so ultimately for an analysis of the human role in the world at large. It seems appropriate, therefore, that the series should also concern itself with those wider anthropological and sociological areas of investigation which, deriving from the linguistic model, ultimately involve scrutiny of the nature of art itself and of its relation to our whole way of life.

This in turn will require attention to be focused on some of those activities which in our society have hitherto been excluded from the prestigious realms of Culture. The disturbing realignment of values which this involves, and the disconcerting nature of the pressures that work to bring it about both constitute areas that *New Accents* will seek to explore.

Each volume in the series will attempt an objective exposition of significant developments in its field up to the present as well as an account of its author's own views of the matter. Each will culminate in an informative bibliography as a guide to further study. And while each will be primarily concerned with matters relevant to its own specific interests, we can hope that a kind of conversation will be heard to develop between them: one whose accents may perhaps suggest the distinctive discourse of the future.

TERENCE HAWKES

INTRODUCTION

THIS book offers a new focus on various connected topics in the treatment of style as a human phenomenon, and especially the style of literary artefacts. The subject of style is of intense and continuing interest, and the bibliography in the field of literary style alone is enormous. The essays that follow are therefore an attempt to contribute to the literature of a continuing study.

Style is sometimes regarded as a comparatively trivial matter, an ornamental excrescence on a meretricious work. Yet style is less a fact of the history of culture than of the history of psychology; it is an indispensable element in communication between one human being and another. As I try to show, the world is impossible to interpret without the phenomenon of style. In a sense, the apprehension of style may be the only function of the human mind. Of the various bearers of style in the arts, the subtle styles of literature are in some ways the most useful to study, as an approach to general style.

Most students of style are conscious of the fact that they are members of a world-wide group. I owe a considerable number of the observations and theoretical approaches in the following pages to long discussions with the late Henry Lee Smith, and with Archibald A. Hill. I also owe a large debt to Randolph Quirk and the members of his seminar on grammar and usage at University College, London, and to the late Aristotle Katranides. Robert Austerlitz, Roger Fowler, Donald Freeman, Morton Bloomfield, Michael Riffaterre, R. A. Sayce, all know what I owe them. Raymond Queneau was a remarkable force in many fields and on many students of style for decades. Finally, two men, Frank Kermode and Terence Hawkes, have been stimulating and provoking influences, sometimes pushing me towards the opinions in these essays, sometimes leading me away from them. The opinions are, of course, mine, but the stimulus to study the nature of style is the result of their influence and that of the contributors to the journal *Language and Style* during my editorship over the past ten years.

1 STYLE AS PERCEPTIVE STRATEGY

STYLE is the regard that *what* pays to *how*.

To human beings the world is full of orders – breathe! drink water! eat food! work! From these iron commands there is no appeal. Yet the amount of freedom outside these commands seems to be immense. Each one of the billions of humans on the earth is distinguishable from the others. Each has a different way of obeying life's commands, a distinctive *how* in respect of the *what* that life consists of, that marks him or her as an individual to fellow humans and to himself or herself.

The *how* of human behaviour, the style, is felt at many levels, from the primitive distinguishing of yourself from everybody – and everything – else, to the identifying of groups of friends and foes, and of men and women (gender itself, a fundamental case of *how*, might be said to be a matter of style). It is perceived in the style of arts and games (the stylish tennis player, the stylish violinist), in fashions (Style with a capital S), and in literature. The basic act of making sense out of the *what* which nature presents to our senses necessarily involves the *how* of style. If style is the man, it is also the world he first constructs and then inhabits.

In this book there will be description only of style in language – a broad area with subtle ramifications – but there is no reason why this method of description cannot be extended to other fields.

I

Style exists on many levels. It distinguishes many degrees of difference.

Early in Huxley's *Point Counter Point*,[1] Lord Edward Tantamount, an experimental biologist, is transplanting the organs of newts in his home laboratory and talking to his assistant, Illidge, about the principles of developmental biology. Downstairs in Lady Edward's party, a chamber orchestra is playing Bach's B minor Suite.

> Diminished and in fragments, the B minor Suite came floating up from the great hall to the ears of the two men in the laboratory. They were too busy to realize that they were hearing it.

Lord Edward begins to talk about the unlikelihood of growth to a definite shape in living creatures:

> 'Growing in a definite shape is very unlikely, when you come to think of it.'

Illidge begins to comment, but Lord Edward's attention is caught by something else.

> But Lord Edward was not listening to his assistant. He had taken his pipe out of his mouth, he had lifted his head and at the same time slightly cocked it on one side. He was frowning, as though making an effort to seize and remember something. He raised his hand in a gesture that commanded silence; Illidge interrupted himself in the middle of his sentence and also listened. A pattern of melody faintly traced itself upon the silence.
> 'Bach?' said Lord Edward in a whisper.

Pongileoni's blowing and the scraping of the anony-mous fiddlers had shaken the air in the great hall, had set the glass of the windows looking on it to vibrating; and this in turn had shaken the air in Lord Edward's apart-ment on the further side. The shaking air rattled Lord Edward's *membrana tympani*, the interlocked *malleus*, *incus*, and stirrup bones were set in motion so as to agitate the membrane of the oval window and raise an infinitesimal storm in the fluid of the labyrinth. The hairy endings of the auditory nerve shuddered like weeds in a rough sea; a vast number of obscure miracles were performed in the brain, and Lord Edward ecstatically whispered 'Bach!' He smiled with pleasure, his eyes lit up.

Lord Edward is beginning to make sense out of a non-laboratory world. As the result of 'a vast number of obscure miracles', he assigns the name of a dead human being to a complex acoustic phenomenon. Human beings, if they are not deaf, live all their lives receiving up to ten thousand bits of information every second through their ears, of which they notice little, and remember less. Although Lord Ed-ward at first did not know that he was hearing the music of Bach, he eventually recognized that he was listening to a type of noise called music, and music once created by an individual whom he can name.

Lord Edward was recognizing *style*, in one form or ano-ther. He may have recognized a fragment of music he had heard before, in which case, if we are not to take refuge in a simple-minded behaviourism, the identification of 'Bach' was in fact a stylistic *reidentification*. A more interesting possibility is that he assigned the name of Bach to a melody he had not heard before, in which case it was a primary act of stylistic judgement. In either case, the phenomenon of stylistic identification had taken place, either in the past or in the present. To understand how this happens we must look at the sort of creatures we are.

All of the senses ceaselessly receive information. A million bits of information enter the eye every second; the skin, the nasal passages, the mouth, the musculature, the semi-circular canals of the ear, all of these constantly experience an unremitting barrage of signals. Even silence is not silent; the collision of molecules of air can occasionally be heard as a shrill hiss. Every time your nerves 'change', you have received 'information'. The condition of the sensory receptors alters rapidly and constantly in the face of this flow, but not even in the eye, the most receptive and responsive of the sensors, can all the stimuli be consciously registered. We ignore vast amounts of information. We notice, or 'apperceive', about ten to twenty bits of information per second out of thousands of millions. A concert pianist, working at top capacity, can notice up to twenty-two bits of visual information per second. However, even this reduced flow is not retained; most people can only retain in their long-term memory the equivalent of two to six bits per second.[2] This adds up to an enormous number of recollections of aural stimuli in a lifetime.

Now, by some mysterious mechanism, Lord Edward had selected from the gigantic number of aural stimuli present in his life a certain set which he can call Bach, and by which he can organize a mass of degenerate and fragmentary data. His feat (one which we all perform every day of our lives) is possible because of the phenomenon of style.

II

Style derives from two fundamental notions that have been loosely characterized above as *what* and *how*: the notions, to be slightly more sophisticated, of some sort of 'base', and of some sort of variation from that base. Both 'stylish' and 'non-stylish' tennis players engage in the sport of tennis in a recognizable form (the *what* or 'base'). They do not, for example, play with a violin for a racket, or insist that let-balls count for scores. If they did so, they would not be playing tennis. Thus, both 'stylish' and 'unstylish' tennis players play the same game according to the same rules. But although an 'unstylish' player may win a great many games, a 'stylish' player also wins admiration and attention at another level. It would seem therefore that the 'stylish' player, in addition to engaging in the minimum 'base' activity of playing tennis, is also perceived as doing something else. It is as if, once the minimum base activity is accomplished, there operates beyond it a set of variations in which the 'stylish' player engages, and which bears additional information to the spectator.

This 'stylistic' activity is often taken to be an expression of the personality of the individual performer. Yet whole teams can have style. The root notion of style, therefore, need not essentially involve individual expression itself, so much as an abstract quality of interpretation, a *double perception* on the part of the observer. The observer perceives an identificative element which establishes the nature of the activity; at the same time he also perceives the stylistic element, the one which distinguishes the *way* in which the activity is performed. This last may convey an impression of personality. Style as a process of interpretation underlies surface distinctions such as content and ornament. As has been suggested above, it is more abstract, a sort of Gestalt schema by which the memory records and indexes its information in terms of *what* and *how*.

So, a man playing tennis 'stylishly' could be perceived in two dimensions:

Identificative dimension (what)	*Stylish dimension (how)*
playing tennis	showing characteristic manner of playing tennis

It is possible to probe behind this notion to a more primitive sort of perception: the act of tennis *itself* can be a 'stylish' act, if the identification is of a more general activity:

Identificative dimension	*Stylish dimension*
human motion	playing tennis

Here the 'non-significant variation' is of the act of human motion; 'playing tennis' is not enough of a variant of human motion to become something other than human motion – it is a *type* of human motion, with governing tenets of its own which are not in conflict with those of human motion.

One may apply this schema even further back, to the most primitive level:

Identificative dimension	*Stylish dimension*
raw sensory information	human motion

Of the myriad impressions received by the senses, some may be combined into an impression of human motion, as opposed to others which provide information about other sorts of phenomena, or are ignored.

It is at this point that we begin to see by what process Lord Edward could begin to notice Bach. Among the 'vast number of obscure miracles' in his brain, a schema of mental organization proceeds hierarchically; it moves from impinging information to reactive information, to apperceived information, to identification as noise, then noise as noise of a certain subtype, then as the creation of one of the creators of music, then as the work of Bach. Schematically, each 'style' acts as the identificative dimension of the succeeding level:

(*a*) *Identificative dimension*	*Stylistic dimension*
acoustic disturbance of the air and the structure of the ear	partial apperceptions from total information

(*b*) *Identificative dimension*	*Stylistic dimension*
partial apperceptions from total information	apperception of part of received information, as music

('They were too busy to realize that they were hearing it.')

('He was frowning, as though making an effort to seize and remember something.')

(c) *Identificative dimension* apperception of part of received information, as music ('A pattern of melody faintly traced itself upon the silence.')

Stylistic dimension recognition as product of specific creator ('Bach?' ... 'Bach!')

The terminal point of this schematic application seems to be where the style perceived is that of an individual, in this case Bach. Even here perhaps we may apply the schema once more:

(d) *Identificative dimension* Bach as Baroque composer

Stylistic dimension Bach as individual

In this final schema we see Bach, a Baroque composer, being a Baroque composer in his own way, Bach's way. Many Baroque composers are never perceived this way – they are the voice of their age and not their own voice. The miracle of personal presence seems to be reserved for the genius and the eccentrics, an overlapping class.

III

The end of the schematic application is the recognition of a human being, an Other, one outside your own perception of the universe. Indeed, perhaps the existential view carries this notion one step further back: in perceiving the irredeemably Other, we perceive Existence itself, an existence distinct from ours. The stylistic search, from the rawest sensorial level to the recognition of exterior existence, seems to be a basic function of the mind; it affirms its own existence by arriving at an acknowledgement of other, exterior, existences.

To perceive our own style is a lifelong task. What is our own characteristic way of being a human being? In our continuous effort to know ourselves we constantly create a 'proto-literature', a 'self'-expression, which we then process as if it were exterior information. We come to know ourselves, that is both 'identificatively' and 'stylistically', by a recycling of memory. As Proust has shown, gustatory and visual memories (madeleines and church towers) can arouse before the mind's eye (and mind's tongue) sensations and emotions which were recorded, as apperceptions or not, of past reality, but which now are 'recycled' as realizations of the content of the memory and hence of the personality. We now *know that we know* these things, and we have a memory of the products of the recycling, which then forms a part of a 'subset' of the memory which is the ego. 'The way I do or say things' is the content of the ego.

While taste, sight, feeling, kinesthesia, balance, and body-extension recyclings and reassignments play a part in the establishment of the ego, the most constant and most subtly modulated input to it is provided by the 'interior monologue'. This internal speech, a sub-auditory stream of aborted articulations, 'egoizes' all our perceptions of outer and inner reality, either immediately, as a stream parallel to the 'stream of consciousness', or as a flow of reminiscence couched in sub-auditory terms. We listen to others to know them; we speak to ourselves to understand ourselves.

Under pressure, the interior monologue may be exteriorized as external speech, or as writing, which may form a type of literary discourse. It is as if the ego can no longer maintain its balance with material from the interior monologue, which passes by the mind's eye too quickly. A more permanent form of self-knowledge, exterior to the mind as if it were an objective fact, is sometimes necessary. Speech and writing can serve this purpose. They seem to give self-know-ledge an objective exterior existence and can thus restore equilibrium to the disturbed system of consciousness. Literary creation, therefore, can be seen to be a heroic, elaborate, and lifelong attempt at self-understanding. By this method, we come to understand the contents of our experience and, more important, our own style in expressing it.

Even here, the stylistic process is in operation. I force myself, the 'irreducible' individual, to penetrate at least two dimensions of schematizing before the truly irreducible ego is discerned.

(a) *Identificative dimension*
my passive long-term
memory acquisitions

Stylistic dimension
recycled contents of my
passive long-term memory,
to form ego

(b) *Identificative dimension*
my ego-content

Stylistic dimension
memory of style of recycled
material, mainly of interior
or exterior monologue
(truly 'my personal style')

Human language functions as the atomizing and linearizing agent by which apperceptions are censored, simplified and ordered into ego-elements, either by interior monologue or by exterior discourse. Human communication is a by-product of this activity – in this model, self-expression and self-knowledge are the primary aims of speech.

We know our own style primarily by observation of the 'auditory streams' of our own internal monologues. We can know the personal styles of others by the nature of their 'auditory streams', mainly discernible by us as different from ours. Other beings are perceived as Other because they are not completely controllable, or perceivable, as extensions of ourselves. If other people's styles were the same as our own, they would be us – *doppelgängers* distinguishable from us in no way that we could discern. To a great extent, it is by means of linguistic style that Otherness becomes noticeable, and our own existence constantly ratified.

The examination of speech and writing for stylistic evidence (of many sorts) is an old pursuit. The phenomenon of stylistic observation has been noted by many critics, from Plato to the present, and each culture notes a different facet or version of it. Seymour Chatman sums up much of the tradition in a recent article, which distinguishes four major definitions of style in writing, all resembling each other in elusive but definite ways.[3]

Chatman's first two types derive from classical and medieval sources. Chatman's 'Definition A' is normative, that is, style is 'good style', a distinguishing characteristic of 'good writing'. 'Definition B' describes style as an objectively distinguishing mark of the individual (rather than a praiseworthy quality of a type of valuable creation): style as 'individual manner'. 'Definition C', which came into English at the end of the sixteenth century, conceives of style an ornamental addition to content, style as *elocutio*. Finally 'Definition D' sees it as 'the verbal reflection of decorum', that is, as the appropriate manner or level of speaking in differing contexts – 'colloquial style', 'formal style', and so on.

These four notions of style obviously have a number of features in common: they present style as a 'secondary' phenomenon, which exists over and above content; they presuppose that style has some positive value, which it adds to content; and they imply of course that style can be analysed, studied (and perhaps even acquired) separately from content.

Since each of these notions concerns itself with the phenomenon of style in relation to written language, it seems appropriate to turn now to linguistic criticism to see what degree of help may be available from that quarter, when it comes to dealing with the manifold relationships of style to content in verse and prose.

2 TYPES OF LINGUISTIC CRITICISM

I

> We must admit the existence of psychological
> doubles of formal grammatical categories.
>   *Lev Vygotsky*[1]

One of the most impressive of Yeats's early poems is *Who Goes with Fergus?* By its intensity and power over language, it stands out from its flocculent neighbours; James Joyce has it play a prominent role in *Ulysses*; one of my teachers, William York Tindall, insisted that all of his students memorize it.

> Who will go drive with Fergus now,
> And pierce the deep wood's woven shade,
> And dance upon the level shore?
> Young man, lift up your russet brow,
> And lift your tender eyelids, maid,
> And brood on hopes and fear no more.
>
> And no more turn aside and brood
> Upon love's bitter mystery;
> For Fergus rules the brazen cars,
> And rules the shadows of the wood,
> And the white breast of the dim sea,
> And all dishevelled wandering stars.

Assuming that the poem deserves special notice among the myriad verse passages of western civilization, what is a critic to say of it? Immediately the great critics and scholars begin to loom from the shades. They proffer information: about the author, about his milieu, about Fergus, about metre and rhyme, about the (presumed) reaction of the (ideal) audience. Finally, the 'formalist' critics proffer information about 'the work itself', which in practice aims at a close description of the way the language of the poem works. If formalist analyses focus upon language, the latest formalists, the linguistic critics, seem to offer tools for the most detailed description of it.

An analysis by a linguistic critic would then proceed explicitly or implicitly on the assumption that there are many effects discernible in the poem which can be traced to the reader's response to the various configurations of language in it. An additional assumption, based on the first, is that the particular excellence of the work derives not from its content, from *what* is said, but either from the abstract deployment of the language itself, or from the closeness of the 'fit' between the content and the linguistic expression of that content: on the *way* in which what is said *is* said. Any 'linguistic' analysis will therefore turn out to be an analysis of style, strictly separating *what* is said from *how* it is said, or, in the terms used above, separating identificative base from stylistic performance.

'Style' here has a number of meanings. It seems to refer to a subjective impression in the reader of the stamp of another personality on the language involved. It also suggests the total effect of the linguistic structures as such, whether they form a portrait of the artist or contribute to the general abstract web of language. Let us see what further, more detailed, comments a linguistic critic might want to make along these lines.

He would note a certain oddness in the language of *Fergus*, as compared to that used in 'ordinary' circumstances.[2]

For instance, it contains a great many repetitions of sound and stress, many more than would occur in casual speech. This, when noted by the reader, identifies it as a poem. However, there are other oddities about it. At first glance there seems to be an excess of conjunctions. What is the function of all those 'ands'? And then, there are a number of ordinarily 'referential' elements which are here free-floating: definite articles with no reference to previous descriptions, addresses to unintroduced personalities, references to undescribed entities. What deep wood? What level shore? Who is Fergus? What young man? What maid? What brazen cars? The speaker of the poem seems to be quite willing to mystify his audience in such matters.

A reader of Yeats's early poetry would be able to say that such vagueness of reference is not simply the characteristic of the speaker of *Fergus* but of most of Yeats's early work. It might perhaps be characteristic of the young Yeats himself. The point might be made that such lack of respect for ordinary principles of topic-definition is a characteristic of certain nineteenth-century schools of poetry – Pre-Raphaelites, Symbolists, Decadents – and conveys a feeling of internality, a notion that the reader is always overhearing an internal discourse of the poet.

But what is *actually* happening? To an ordinarily sensitive reader the focus of the poem seems diffuse. The putative 'frame of mind' of the speaker is only negatively described by saying that the speaker seems willing to mystify the reader. The poem consists of questions, commands, and strong assertions. Why then is the effect so mild and Pre-Raphaelite? Why does the speaker's mind seem to be on something other than what he is saying? And why have the questions and imperatives in the poem the mitigated authority of the gestures of Beardsley figures?

A linguistic critic might begin his analysis of these matters by asking: what is a question, or a command, or an assertion? There has been a great deal of recent work on the conditions that define the asking of a true question, the issuing of a true command, the declaration of a truly intended assertion, following the lead of John Austin and John Searle and their description of the nature of 'speech acts' and 'illocutionary force'.[3] The 'illocutionary force' of an utterance lies in its intended *use*; the locution achieves its end only if its 'constitutive conditions' are satisfied. The constitutive conditions are different for the asking of 'true' questions, as opposed to rhetorical questions, examination questions, or riddles, to say nothing of locutions which have the form of questions without their force, such as 'Why don't you go jump in the lake?'

Searle describes the conditions for the asking of true questions as follows:

(a) The questioner does not have the information necessary to complete a proposition truly.

(b) It is not obvious to the questioner and his audience that the audience will provide the information without being asked.

(c) The questioner wants the information.

(d) The question counts as an attempt to elicit information.[4]

The complex question under examination – 'Who will go drive with Fergus now / And pierce the deep wood's woven shade, / And dance upon the level shore?' – 'fails' as a true question by the absence of an immediately present audience, which seems to violate conditions (b) and (d). All written questions, with the exception of those in personal letters and government forms, would fail as true questions for these reasons. (In fact, Richard Ohmann has suggested that it is a general characteristic of literature at large, that the locutions that comprise it have *all* lost their illocutionary force in order to acquire the force specifically of literary locutions.[5])

With this evidence that the question in lines 1–3 of *Fergus* is not a 'true' question, it becomes necessary to ask what it is, and to see if the answer is valuable for a critical description of the poem's style.

The game principle

There is, as I suggested above, a general stylistic effect of mild absent-mindedness in the poem, the sense of a sort of double or contrapuntal mental 'set'. The denial of *all* illocutionary force to the question in lines 1–3 would not convey this complex impression, at least by itself; the (written) questions in Blake's *Tyger*, for instance, convey quite a different impression.[6] The generalized loss of illocutionary force by written or literary questions is not a genuine loss. It is as if the poet and the reader are playing a literary game in which the 'penalty' for violating the laws of asking true questions is the establishment of a limited situation. In that situation the process of asking and answering questions can only be imitated. The same rules apply *within* the imitative game, however, as in the non-literary context. The result of the game is not a true answering of questions but *an observing of the asking of them*, and the same would be true of imperatives and assertions: within the literary game, the reader observes the poet commanding and asserting, without feeling bound to obey or believe. However, since within the game the rules for asking questions, making commands or asserting are still being 'obeyed', we can use the linguist's tools to examine *Fergus*, as if we were analysing casual speech; we will always return at the end, however, to the moderated form of the language established by the literary game.

Illocutionary force can usually be determined clearly only by consultation with context, both linguistic and extra-linguistic. However, there are certain syntactic elements which inherently can have no place in either questions or commands, if these are to remain 'purely' questioning or commanding. These are the so-called 'non-restrictive modifiers', of which non-restrictive adjectives and relative clauses are the most commonly described type. In Othello's command 'keep up your bright swords or the dew will rust them' (I. ii. lines 58–9), the adjective 'bright' is non-restrictive, a type of parenthetical observation, with a definite 'by-the-way' feeling about it. (The context must make it clear, of course, that the 'bright swords' are not being contrasted, restrictively, with dull ones.) Another of Othello's commands, 'Silence that dreadful bell!' (II. iii. line 166) contains a non-restrictive modifier, 'dreadful', and is therefore not a 'pure' command. 'Dreadful' adds an effective note of irritation, but is not strictly necessary for the command; there is only one bell to silence, and thus no need to define it further. Mitigated commands are common in casual speech, so their use in poetry is not unprecedented. However for a full description of their effect we need to examine both their nature and their function.

When the speaker in *Fergus* observes the depth of the wood, the weaving of the shade, the levelness of the shore, and so on, he appears to be engaged in mental acts which take the linguistic form of non-restrictive acts of attribution. However, the surface evidence of these acts – 'deep', 'woven', 'level', 'russet', 'tender', 'bitter', 'brazen', 'white', 'dim', 'dishevelled' (and perhaps 'wandering', which may, however, be restrictive) – are all embedded in sentences which serve other illocutionary functions than that of simple attribution, in that they are questions and commands. The mental stance for a 'pure' command, as for a true question, does not possess the self-informative quality of the act of attribution. Questions confess ignorance and a drive for externally supplied information: they imply a *future*, when puzzles will be solved. Commands also contain (implicit) references to a future state, a state more satisfactory to the commander than the present. Attributives, however, refer to the *past*, in which the evidence for the attribution has been gathered. These ten or eleven non-restrictive attributes, therefore, modify and mitigate the questions in the poem (within the game), by dragging down the future force of questions and commands.

Question	Assertions
Who will go drive with	the woods are deep
Fergus now, and pierce the	the shade looks as if
wood's shade?	someone had woven it.

This introduction of non-restrictive 'impurities' is a primary source for the feeling of diffuseness and lack of definite focus in *Fergus*. The linguist is able here to point to the means by which the speaker of the poem seems to be lingering in the present and past whilst at the same time striving to affect the future. The poetic game is here played with the asking of questions, issuing of commands, and making of assertions – all of which are mitigated, in themselves and in context.

The use of linguistic techniques to provide criticism with additional tools of analysis is one type of description of style. Here the tools have helped us analyse Yeats's style, though at this point no distinction has been made between the analysis of the 'poetic' use of general language, in a game, and the description of the intensely personal element in Yeats's use of language. As we will see, this second 'personal' sort of analysis is based firmly on the first, for to be able to describe particular patterns of linguistic habits in the work of individuals, a close description of these habits must be available.

II

In describing the relationship between thought and language, the Russian psycholinguist Lev Vygotsky described language as the culmination of a series of internal psychological processes.

The word forms the end and not the beginning of the

development. The word is the end which crowns the deed.[7]

In another place, Vygotsky compared thought to 'a cloud shedding a shower of words'.[8] Both of these views find in language the most intimate possible revelation of prior internal mental states. An examination of linguistic 'output' should, therefore, reveal some imprint of those deeply personal aspects of style which preceded and moulded it.

Richard Ohmann, in a well-known essay,[9] has put forward a hypothesis that personal literary style can be described, at least in part, by examination of the characteristic idiosyncratic choice of syntactic structures employed by the author. For example, he finds in D. H. Lawrence constant and characteristic features of repetition and reduction; in the following passage from *Studies in Classic American Literature*, Ohmann discerns the obsessive personality of Lawrence emerging as an aspect of his style:

> The renegade hates life itself. He wants the death of life. So do these many 'reformers' and 'idealists' who glorify the savages in America. They are death-birds, life-haters. Renegades.
> We can't go back. And Melville couldn't. Much as he hated the civilized humanity he knew. He couldn't go back to the savages. He wanted to. He tried to. And he couldn't. Because in the first place it made him sick.

When Ohmann examines this passage, which features a high degree of elision, he finds it possible to reconstruct some of the syntactic elements which by their combination produce the passage, as well as the abbreviative conventions that disguise the extreme obsessive repetitiveness of the whole. With the restoration of the elided elements, the passage reads:

> The renegade hates life itself. He wants the death of life.

So do these many 'reformers' and 'idealist' who glorify the savages in America [want the death of life]. They are death-birds. [They are] life-haters. [They are] renegades.

We can't go back. And Melville couldn't [go back]. [Melville couldn't go back, as] much as he hated the civilized humanity he knew. He couldn't go back to the savages. He wanted to [go back to the savages]. He tried to [go back to the savages]. And he couldn't [go back to the savages].

Another aspect of this type of analysis deals with the characteristic choice of words rather than syntactic units. In the passage from Lawrence, there seems to be a deliberate attempt to choose words for their shock value, in the place of their more decorous and abstract synonyms. The passage would read very differently if for 'savages' we substituted the currently fashionable phrase 'non-technologically advanced peoples'. Use of abstraction or euphemism (or its opposite, dysphemism, for that matter) seems to be as much a personal stylistic trait as a social one.

There are other possible sorts of 'personal' stylistic characterization through language. For example, a typically 'logical' order to discourse by topic and subtopic, even in a casual context, can characterize a person to those of his hearers who are sensitive to such rhetorical clarity. He may also be distinguished by choice of topic, as well as the appropriateness (or the reverse) of the topic to the context chosen. In this case both the topic itself and the speaker's sense of congruity to social surroundings are factors in a judgement of style. In addition to these internal linguistic factors, there are those which depend upon external physical 'givens', the physical signs of individual style: quality of voice, appearance and deployment of physical appearance and 'body-set', idiosyncratic penmanship, and the like. Every aspect of descriptive linguistics – graphemics, kinesics, paralanguage, phonology, syntax, semantics, rhetoric, sociolinguistics and psycholinguistics, among others – is capable of distinguishing style.

Literary style, like all style, reveals both the individual personality of the creator and the general language habits of the society in which he lives. To see how such a double focus is possible, we should examine our ways of interpreting the evidence of our senses – our public and private strategies of perception.

3 PLAYING THE LITERATURE GAME: A PUBLIC AND COLLECTIVE NORM

Public and private games

As I have suggested above, tennis is a 'style' of human motion, and is distinguished from general motion by its own rules. However, there are also individually 'stylish' players. The same is true of literature. It is distinguished from general vocal or written expression by those *ways of operating* or of *being regarded* that are peculiar to the literary game. Yet there are also individual styles of writing.

From the beginnings of literary analysis as we know it, in Greece, these two sorts of analysis of stylistic perceptions – distinguishing activities and distinguishing individuals: public and private styles – have woven in and out of each other. The Greeks were well aware of the distinction between content and style, but their attitude towards these familiar abstractions were not quite ours. Rhetoricians from Plato and Aristotle to Protagoras and Demetrius distinguished *dianoia* or *pragmata* ('thought' or 'facts') from *lexis* and *taxis* ('word-choice' or 'arrangement'). They expertly distinguished the characteristic lexical and tactical configurations of Demosthenes and Sophocles among others, not descriptively, in order to differentiate between them as *individual* creators, but prescriptively, to set out the rules of

style. It almost seems as if Demosthenes' individual peculiarities of style were seen not as personal tics but counted as
ways of playing the 'oratory game' which others had better
learn. The style of Demosthenes was not his personal or
distinctive brand of speaking but the way to be an orator – a
Platonic ideal of the orator revealing itself in gleams of
Style through the individual activity of Demosthenes. In
our day the closest parallel to this way of interpreting personal style as public tenet can be found in chess. The 'personal' idiosyncrasies of Morphy, Steinitz, Tarrasch, Niem-
zovitch, Capablanca, Alekhine and others turn out to be
ways of playing the game that the game itself requires. It is
the notion 'oratory' or the notion 'chess' that becomes
clearer, not the notion 'Demosthenes' or the notion 'Niem-
zovitch'.

The idea of a public game – the revealing of 'oratory',
'tragedy', 'comedy', 'history', through the activity and
peculiarities of its practitioners – soon gave way to the
notion of privacy familiar to the Romantics and to us,
namely, that of the utterly private idiosyncrasies of individuals. There seems to have been a retreat inwards ac-
companying the conquest of Greece by the Macedonians.
The fourth-century Hellenistic poet Callimachus wrote: 'I
hate the cycle poems [epics], and view with no joy a road
which carries many men here and there . . . All public
things disgust me.' Under the Macedonians in Greece and,
later on, in Rome under the decaying Republic and the
Empire, the public games of statehood were being played
for the citizens, not *by* them. The experts in statecraft took
over from ordinary people, and public participation in
government gave way to government as a 'spectator sport',
with an audience watching the heroes of civil war and military anarchy battle it out. The nature of the game itself was
settled by impersonal 'professional' authority. Style was to
become the sum of the ways in which an individual player
might play it. The Roman distinction between *facta* and

stilus, things and the style of things, *what* and *how*, is partly the distinction of the individual reactions of human beings under pressure, when all that human beings have in common are their differences. (The official Roman 'line' emphasized the collective, but the modern reader can recognize the presence of individual styles in the great Roman creators.)

Since that time stylistic study has had two main objectives: to describe the nature of both the public games of style and of private styles.

The first concern, the study of the public games of literature, leads the critic to try to describe how literary creators employ the linguistic codes they and their hearers and readers possess *completely or partially in common*. The emphasis here is on similarities of code, not differences; therefore, the effects described reside potentially in the standard language. Here, on the Greek model mentioned above, it is 'literature' that is becoming clearer, not 'writers'.

The second concern is not with the potentialities of a public, collective norm of language at all but with the description of private styles, with the reasons for a reader's intuition of *individual* personality in literary and other stretches of utterance. This approach pursues style to its last division, to the centre of personality itself, and is, therefore, rather more along the line of the Roman model above, an examination of an intensely *private* deployment of linguistic possibilities.

Let us begin with the public game, and its most 'public' aspect. A literary creator makes use of all the components of the linguistic apparatus that he and his audience possess in common. This may include a private stylistic component (everybody has one), but it certainly includes all of the 'public' components of language. They involve *phonology* – the poet and the audience share sound-systems and systems of intonation – and *syntax*. To say this is to say only that the poet and his audience speak the same language.

The public game I: the sound patterns of poetry

Poets use the characteristic motions used for the pronunciation of sounds for artistic purposes. We can all feel that the tongue lies at the bottom of the mouth in the pronunciation of 'aw!' and 'ah!' and humps itself up higher and higher in 'ed', 'ad', and 'id'. In 'id' the tension is considerable, and can be augmented by a forced smiling, a stretching of the lips. If we are carefully performing a line (of poetry or not) in which the stressed syllables range from 'aw' to 'id', we can be made to force the tongue higher and higher, and more and more forward in the buccal cavity of the mouth, and to force the lips wider and wider apart:

AW	AH	ED	AD	ID
Or	f*a*r	ev*e*nts	*a*dd	*i*nterest.

The movements of the tongue here do not add anything to the appreciation of the sentence, since the sense of the sentence has nothing to do (except vaguely) with 'moving upward'. In a sentence like the following, perhaps inserted in a poem about climbing a hill, the movement of the stressed vowels does have a descriptive (or mimetic) value:

AW	AH	ED	AD	ID
S*o*rely	tr*i*ed,	*e*verybody	cl*a*mbered to the tip

(Note that the 'tried' begins its vowel sounds with 'ah' before moving to 'ee'.)

Poets have been aware of the possibilities of reinforcing meaning with sound ever since Homer (and probably before). It has always seemed an added grace of style (onomatopoeia) when the sound seems an echo to the sense. But what actually happens in these cases?

Let us have a closer look at some lines in which the poets 'force' an articulation pattern on the reader as part of their public stylistic repertoire.

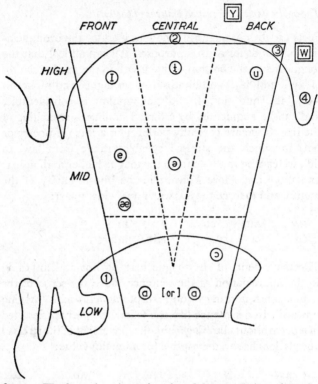

figure 1: The buccal cavity or interior of the mouth (seen from the side) and possible positions of the vowels and glides (Standard American [E. L. Epstein])

1. Tongue
2. Hard palate ('y' glide)
3. Soft palate ('velum') ('w' glide)
4 Uvula

High-front: 'I' as in 'bit' or 'id'
Mid-front: 'e' as in 'bet' or 'bear' or 'ed'; 'æ' as in 'bat' or 'ad'
Low-front: 'a' as in 'pot' or 'bog' or *Low-back* or 'ah!'

Low-back: 'ɔ' as in 'bought' or 'horse' or 'aw'
High-back: 'u' as in 'put' or 'good'
Mid-central: 'ə' as in 'butt'
High-central: 'ɨ' as in 'church'

Note: This chart represents a compromise and simplification of many systems, and is based upon a description of Standard American Speech in G. L. Trager, and H. L. Smith, Jr., *An Outline of English Structure*, Norman, Oklahoma, 1951. Some systems place 'æ' as low and 'ɔ' as mid.

Take the following examples:

(a) [Weep no more, woeful shepherds, weep no more,
     For Lycidas, your sorrow, is not dead,]
     Sunk though he be beneath the watry floor.
                              (Milton, *Lycidas*)

(b) A lonely impulse of delight
     Drove to this tumult in the clouds
                              (Yeats, *An Irish Airman*)

(c) The roll, the rise, the carol, the creation
                              (Hopkins, *To R. B.*)

(d) A bracelet of bright hair about the bone.
                              (Donne, *The Relic*)

(e) The fine delight that fathers thought.
                              (Hopkins, *To R. B.*)

(f) Accomplished fingers begin to play.
     Their eyes mid many wrinkles, their eyes,
     Their ancient, glittering eyes, are gay.
                              (Yeats, *Lapis Lazuli*)

Selections (a), (b), and perhaps (c) seem to refer to *actual* movements in space. Selections (d) and (e) seem to display a metaphorical, emotional 'movement', while selection (f) sustains a certain feeling of buoyancy. It is possible that the sound-structure of the lines (specifically, the pattern derived from comparing the stressed vowels of each line), either *reinforces* or *produces* the effects referred to (see figure 1).

In pronouncing the *stressed* vowels in selection (a). 'Sunk though he be beneath the watry floor', the tongue-muscle mimes a movement from low-mid to high-front to low-back in the mouth, as any reader can feel for himself by observing the movements of the tongue:

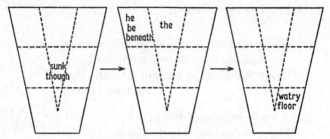

figure 2: Vowel positions in the line from *Lycidas*

The 'buccal dance', as the French critic André Spire calls it, reinforces the meaning of line (*a*); the surface of the sea seems to be mimed by the high-front vowels ('be', 'beneath'), and the vowels placed between low or low-back stressed vowels ('sunk', 'watry', 'floor'), seem to convey a notion of the bottom of the sea. Of course, it cannot be said too often that content always precedes pronunciation; as Pope insisted, the sound must seem an *echo* to the sense.*

In selection (*b*), 'A lonely impulse of delight', the situation is less directly mimed. In the lines from *Lycidas* the stressed vowels in 'sunk' and 'watry floor' are actually *below* the points of articulation for 'be' and '-neath'. The first and last vowels stressed in the lines from *An Irish Airman* – 'lone-' and '-light' – demand a tongue-movement from low to high (miming the aeroplane climbing) using a more complex pattern which involves diphthongs (see figure 3):

As the reader can feel, the vowel material in 'lone-' begins with a mid-central vowel and *glides* to a sound

---

* It is still an open question, however, as to whether the articulations necessary to perform a line of verse are actually operative in silent reading. No reading is entirely silent, of course; the tongue muscle flexes during silent reading as if preparing for speech. In addition, the 'motor theory of perception' suggests that a reader or listener mimes mentally the articulatory action, actual or potential, of the speaker to whom he is listening, or of the writer of the line he is reading. For a treatment of the topic of the 'buccal dance', see Delbouille, P., *Poésie et Sonorités* (Paris: Société d'Edition 'Les Belles Lettres', 1961), pp. 57–69.

pronounced in the same place and in approximately the same way as the sound 'w', that is, with the back of the tongue pressed against the back of the mouth (the soft palate, or velum), and the lips pursed. The material in '-light' begins lower and (perhaps) further back in the mouth than the vowel in 'lone-', but glides to a sound articulated

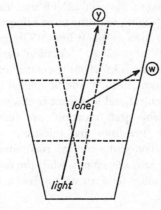

figure 3: The stressed vowels beginning and ending the line from Yeats's *Irish Airman*

like 'y', with the tongue pressed against the hard palate, at a point in front, and slightly above, the point of velar articulation for the 'w' glide; here the lips are stretched in a smile:

lone-	*-light*	(ordinary spelling)
'ləwn'	'layt'	(phonemic notation)
velar glide	palatal glide	

Although the point of articulation for 'y' is slightly higher than that of 'w', it seems to be the movement *forward* in the point of articulation, from the soft palate to the hard palate, that symbolizes the movement *upward* of the aeroplane. Perhaps, paradoxically, the greater distance in the movement required to produce '-light' than to produce 'lone-', a movement beginning at a lower point, also helps to produce a subjective impression in the reader of an upward movement. (Robert Frost performs the same movement, with the same effect, in his line 'The *road* at the top of the *rise*' in *The Middleness of the Road*.)

In the selection (*c*), 'The roll, the rise, the carol, the creation', the vowel material in 'roll' and 'rise' is the same as in 'lone-' and '-light', with the same subjective effect. (Note also the alliteration in these lines.) The greater rise from 'roll' and 'rise' to 'carol' and 'creation' derives partly from the actual *difference in height* of the vowels, and partly from a movement *forward*; both 'ə' and 'a' are low or central in the mouth (mid-central and low-front/back), while the stressed vowels in 'carol' and 'creation' are further *forward* or actually *higher* (low-front and mid-front – gliding to the hard palate). The glides outline two separate patterns of 'upward' (forward) movement, while the vowels 'recoil' and then move steadily forward and upward, for a single expressive curve:

roll	rise	ca(rol)	(cre)a(tion)
'əw'	'ay'	'æ'	'ey'

vowels: mid-central→low-front/back→mid-front

(rise expressed)

glides: velar→palatal→none→palatal
(rise expressed)   (rise expressed)

Note also that in 'creation', the vowel material of the weakly stressed first syllable nevertheless possesses a 'ɪy' articulation, ending on the hard palate, which is then repeated for the following, stressed, syllable, 'krɪyéyšin'. The complex buccal dance of the tongue journeying swiftly upward and forward to articulate the line mimes the content of the line, the metaphorical downward roll and upward rise, perhaps miming the skylark of the poet's thought. (Again, however, if the line expressed a *different* idea than that of upward expanding movement, such a sound pattern as the above would be irrelevant, if not actually contradictory; content is logically and psychologically primary.) (See figure 4.)

In selection (*e*), 'The fine delight that fathers thought', 'fine' and 'delight' glide to a 'bright' (i.e. forward) palatal articulation; then the line becomes grave with the low or mid-back, glideless vowels of '*fathers*' and '*thought*'): ay, ay, a, ɔ. Indeed, Hopkins may have pronounced 'thought' as 'θat' rather than 'θɔt', so all four stressed vowels would be the same, 'a'; the effect of the line would depend upon the pensive mood which is evoked when the low vowel, 'a', is deprived of its 'bright' glide, 'y'.

In addition to the dance of the tongue muscle, the actual or potential movements of the lips in the physical or mental articulation of a poetic line frequently provides significant dramatic reinforcement of the effect of the line's meaning. The pronunciation of front vowels in English is often assisted by a 'smiling' (unrounded) motion of the lips ('bit', 'bet', 'bat'), while vowels like 'u' in 'put', and the velar glide 'w' sometimes require a pursing or rounding of the lips. In effect, a poet frequently forces you to smile or frown when you pronounce his lines. Donne does, in selection (*d*), 'A bracelet of bright hair about the bone', for two of the first three stressed syllables. The simple vowels (apart from glides) in 'brace-' and 'hair' are both front vowels (in my pronunciation almost the same vowel, 'e', as in 'pet'), and both force me to smile. The glides in 'brace-' and 'bright' are both the high, hard-palate glide 'y', so by the combination of front vowels and front glides, the first three stressed syllables are all 'bright' (i.e. forward) in articulatory movement. Then 'bone' alters everything; a mid-central vowel gliding to the velum (with a pursing of the lips) switches off the light. Here there is no actual movement expressed in the content, either that of the mind's eye in *Lycidas* seeking

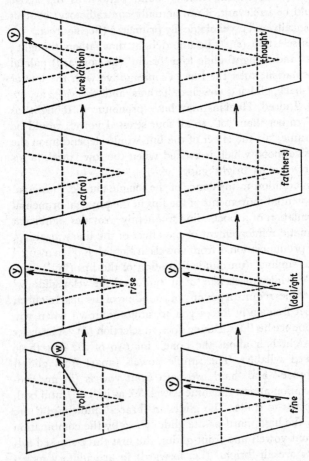

figure 4: The vowel movement in the Hopkins lines from *To R. B.*

Edward King beneath the surface of the Irish Sea, or of an airman or skylark-poet rising to a height. The 'movement' is essentially metaphorical, a sudden sinking of the spirit from the smiling notions of 'bracelet' and 'bright hair' to the grimness of 'bone'.

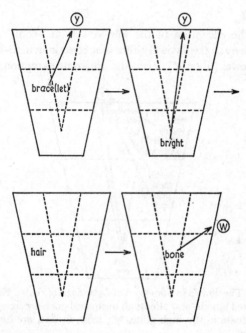

figure 5: The stressed vowels in Donne's line 'a bracelet of bright hair about the bone'

When the poet forces the reader physically to smile or look grave, the appropriate emotion is also often evoked or reinforced. In the lines from *Lapis Lazuli*, Yeats conveys the 'gaiety' of the disciplined attitude to tragedies (the theme of the poem) by the buccal dance of the stressed syllables (in my pronunciation):

accomplished	a	wrinkles	I
fingers	I	eyes	ay
begin	I	ancient	ey
play	ey	glittering	I
eyes	ay	eyes	ay
many	e	gay	ey

With the exception of the low vowels in '-com-' and in 'eyes', *every* stressed vowel either is or contains a high- or mid-front vowel ('I' or 'e'); even the apparent exception, 'ay' in

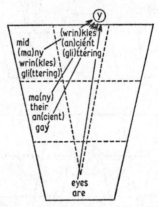

figure 6: The vowels in lines 54–6 of *Lapis Lazuli* (Yeats). Note that all stressed vowels, and almost all unstressed ones, are front vowels or eventuate in the high glide, 'y'; most, in fact, are high- and mid-front.

'eyes', may originate in a low-front vowel and then glide up to the hard palate, as 'ay'. Many of the unstressed syllables are also high- or mid-front: 'accomplished', 'fingers', 'begin', 'their', 'mid', 'many', 'wrinkles', 'ancient', 'glittering' (see figure 6). There is, therefore, a generally 'bright', high tone, accompanied by almost constant smiling, a steady gaiety.

This is not an accident; Yeats when he wishes can orchestrate vowels in an entirely different area, for an entirely different effect. Consider his deployment of *low* vowels in his own epitaph:

Cast a cold eye
On life, on death,
Horseman, pass by.

The vowel in the word 'eye' here fits into a trio of lines that contain no high-front vowels at all, and in which most are very low. It looks as if Yeats, by emphasizing or avoiding buccal areas, could control vowel register with great sensitivity for the strong emotional reinforcement of content.

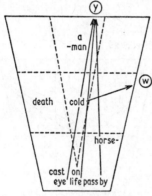

figure 7: The vowels in Yeats's epitaph (in my pronunciation)

Sometimes an entire poem features mainly low or mid vowels, as in Yeats's epitaph, for a mimesis of impressive 'chest' speech. Kipling's *Recessional* is such a poem. The first stanza shows the tongue sunk on the floor of the mouth, or only rising part way, thus allowing a resonance to be projected from the chest. Note that the only high stressed vowel occurs in 'dom*i*nion' (and possibly in 'ben*e*ath – if that is a stressed vowel):

God of our fathers, known of old,
Lord of the far-flung battle-line,
Beneath whose awful hand we hold

Dominion over palm and pine,
Lord God of hosts, be with us yet,
Lest we forget, lest we forget!

This pattern (see figure 8) is sustained throughout the poem, the only prominent exception being the contrast at 'reeking tube' – the vocal trace of the hysterical pride of the enemy, perhaps.*

Once this type of vocal orchestration is mastered, a poet

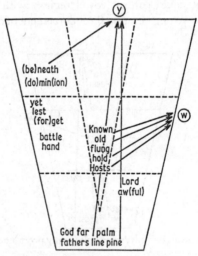

figure 8: The stressed vowels in the first stanza of Kipling's *Recessional*

in control of his craft can write (or rewrite) a sonorous poem of this sort with considerable assurance that it will succeed in its effect. Indeed, the opposite effect can be obtained by avoiding these low and mid vowels. It is almost as if our

---

* Note that Pope orchestrates the last six lines of *The Dunciad*, Bk. IV, in exactly the same way. The reader can work out the vowel pattern for himself, and will find that almost all of the stressed vowels, and many of the unstressed ones, in these powerful lines are mid vowels or very low, and very grave. Except, appropriately enough, for 'glimpse', there are no high-front vowels at all.

emotions are reactions to what our body is doing, as in the well-known theory of emotion associated with William James: 'I am weeping, therefore I must be unhappy.' The reader's version of this theory would be: 'I am pronouncing deep, sonorous sounds, therefore I must be in deadly earnest.'

We have now seen reinforcement of content by buccal miming in several lines. However, buccal movement is by no means always directly mimetic. It may be purely ornamental. Tennyson, for example, seems to delight in abstract buccal exercises, as in *Tithonus*:

The woods decay, the woods decay and fall.
The vapours weep their burthen to the ground.
Man comes and tills the field and lies beneath,
And after many a summer dies the swan.
Me only cruel immortality
Consumes; I wither slowly in thine arms,
Here at the quiet limit of the world,
A white-haired shadow, roaming like a dream,
The ever-silent spaces of the East,
Far-folded mists and gleaming halls of morn.

There seems to be little echoing of content here, except perhaps in the sixth and seventh lines, and in 'fall' and 'burthen'. On the contrary, the vowel patterning seems to operate on its own, and even tends to de-emphasize the specific message. It is almost as if Tennyson were more interested in his own vocal apparatus than in his themes – a suspicion that many critics have voiced.

The public game II: intonation

The above analysis has treated only one aspect of phonology, and that in only one way. The descriptions of sounds have emphasized their actually present or mentally envisaged methods of production ('articulation'). The description of effects produced by syllable articulation is, however, only the beginning of a description of the styles of language in the literature game. The articulatory pattern for the pronunciation of syllables is frequently overridden by an intonational pattern, one that provides possible pronunciations for sentences and discourses, and which is only indirectly linked to a syllable-by-syllable schematic analysis.

There is no more confused or controversial area in linguistics than the description of intonation (or 'prosody', as it is frequently termed by British linguists). The phenomenon of intonation is obvious enough; with careful pronunciation it indicates the difference between these two sentences:

(a) Seven days make one week.
(b) Seven days make one weak.

Intonation seems to be a matter of pitch, of pauses, and of varying stress on syllables. (From here on, internal pauses in the sentence will be indicated by vertical lines (|); the straight or curved lines above the sentence indicate the movement of the pitch intonation.) For example, sentence (a) could reasonably be intoned:

(a) Seven-days|make|one-week.

Sentence (b) could be intoned:

(b) Seven-days|make-one|weak.

If sentence (a), which seems to mean 'a week is made up of seven days', were to be intoned in sentence (b)'s pattern, it would sound bizarre: the speaker would seem to be hesitating and then speeding ahead, as if under the influence of strong emotion. If sentence (b), which seems to mean 'seven days [of dissipation] leave the reveller in a debilitated condition', were intoned like sentence (a), it would seem even stranger; perhaps the entire meaning would be lost.

The intonational situation, however, is not at all as clear-

cut and obvious as these examples would suggest. Sentences
(a) and (b) are 'segmentally homophonic'; that is, intonation apart, they contain the same sounds in the same order
(or similar sounds: weaker stress often alters vowel quality).
Yet most sentences in casual discourse are not ambiguous in
the ways these sentences are. Even if they were, there is a
good chance that the distinction between them would not be
due to clear intonation; most people would simply rely upon
context to resolve the ambiguity. As we will see, intonation
is to a certain (or uncertain) extent unnecessary for meaning. The function of intonation seems to be to *reinforce*
syntactic and semantic guesses already entertained by the
listener to such utterances, rather than to *signal* the primary
information to the listener, as to an entirely passive recip-
ient.

This realization has caused a complete alteration in the
study of modern phonology. To those linguists who believe
that listeners are mere passive recipients of sets of acoustic
signals which bear all the necessary information for their
decoding and interpretation, this sloppiness of normal intonational standards is highly distressing and has led to
considerable hypothesizing that has not stood up very well
to objective testing. In one test, two linguists have made
widely varying transcriptions of the same utterances, many
of their markings corresponding to no part of the actual
acoustic events, as measured by a recording machine. This
has led one diligent investigator of intonational phenomena,
Philip Lieberman, to conclude that 'competent linguists do
not consider simply the physically present acoustic signal'
when they transcribe the intonational phenomena that they
think they have heard.[1] Lieberman suggests a more complex
hypothesis:

The listener mentally constructs a phonetic signal that in-
corporates both the distinctive features that are uniquely
categorized by the acoustic signal and those that he

hypothesized in order to arrive at a reasonable syntactic and semantic interpretation of the message. In some instances the acoustic signal may be both necessary and sufficient to specify uniquely the phonetic elements of the message. This usually occurs when a talker is asked to read aloud nonsense syllables or isolated words. The talker, of course, 'knows' that the message will not allow the listener to test any reasonably complex phonetic hypotheses. The speaker therefore carefully articulates the message.

The speaker's decisions on the relative precision with which he must specify the phonetic elements of the message in the acoustic signal must be made in some interpretive component of the grammar. The speaker must weigh the anticipated linguistic competence of the hearer as well as the linguistic context furnished by the entire sentence, the semantic context of the social situation . . . The listener's process of phonetic hypothesis formation also takes place in this interpretive component . . .[2]

While this hypothesis may explain the comparative lack of intonational structures in the acoustic texture of casual conversation, the situation appears to be different for the silent reader of poetry. Here the speaker is his own listener, and there is some evidence that externally or internally articulated intonation in such a situation conventionally acquires a crystalline perfection rare in less limited contexts. This perfection is described by Martin Joos, in *The Five Clocks*, as a feature of 'formal style':

Lacking all personal support, the text must fight its own battles . . . Robbed of personal links to reality . . . it endeavours to employ only logical links . . . The pronunciation [intonation] is explicit to the point of clattering . . .[3]

This formal style applies to the silent reading of poetry, since here indeed 'the text must fight its own battles'. In addition, normally unnecessary intonational devices (stress, pitch, juncture) are *not* unnecessary in the performance of literary artefacts, since such specifically literary phenomena as metre, rhythm, cesura, balance, rhetorical emphasis and the like may and normally do depend upon a 'clatteringly explicit' performance.

Pope provides an excellent example of the extent to which poets rely upon their readers' sense of 'formal style' to intone their poems adequately (more adequately, in many cases, than the poets themselves, who tend to be wretched performers of their own work; after all, it is old stuff to them!). In *An Essay on Criticism* (1711), there is a famous poetic *jeu d'esprit*, a series of more than four dozen lines (lines 337–93) on the errors of Pope's contemporaries and his prescriptions for improvement. In these lines he defines faults and virtues, demonstrating them at the same time with what the eighteenth century called 'representative metre' (imitative effects). Although these lines are a mine for the linguistic critic, a magnificent example of playing the public literature game, I propose to analyse only one couplet, a famous one:

> When *Ajax* strives, some Rock's vast Weight to throw,
> The Line too *labours*, and the Words move *slow* . . .

There is no doubt here as to Pope's intentions – the effect has been clear to more than two hundred and sixty years of readers. Pope himself wrote: '. . . a good Poet will adapt the very Sounds, as well as Words, to the Things he treats of. So that there is (if one may express it so) a Style of Sound . . .' As we shall see, the 'Style of Sound' Pope describes involves more than the individual sounds themselves (the 'segmental phonemes'), and their transitional peculiarities. The more important effects are conveyed by the intonational phenomena forced upon the reader by the poet, and as Pope says in the same letter: 'This . . . is undoubtedly of wonderful force in imprinting the image on the reader.'[4]

The slow tempo and 'obstruction' in the reading of the Ajax lines are obviously meant by Pope to mime the difficulty of the feat described, the manipulation of a huge rock by the Grecian warrior, as, for example, in Book XII, line 383, of the *Iliad*.*

The Ajax lines have often been analysed, but the sources of the effect of obstruction and difficulty obvious to the reader have never been completely or precisely described. It turns out that an adequate description requires a theory of articulation and intonation which is only now in the process of formulation, and is the subject of fierce debate. However, there are a few immediately discernible causes of these effects. For instance, there is what seems to be the substitution of spondees (two strong stresses) for iambic feet (one weak followed by one strong stress) in the third and fourth feet in the first line, and for the second and fifth feet in the second line (to compensate, pyrrhic feet – two weak stresses – are substituted for the third foot of the second line):

> When Ájăx strives, sóme Róck's vást Wéight tŏ thrów,
> Thĕ Líne tóo lăbŏurs, ănd thĕ Wórds móve slŏw . . .

Yet to refer the obstruction to spondees and pyrrhic feet is to appeal from one mystery to another, for we may well ask why we are forced to pronounce the obstructive spondees and pyrrhic feet where they occur, and how do we know that they are occurring?

It is first necessary to dismiss the notion that the obstructive effect of the Ajax lines is caused by the number of sounds in them that are 'hard to pronounce'. All of the individual sounds in the line are English sounds, and therefore there

---

* See also *Iliad* VII, lines 268–9; in the translation of these lines made (or overseen) by Pope, there is a rather feeble attempt at the effect of lifting and heaving a boulder:
> He poiz'd, and swung it round: then lost on high,
> It flew with Force, and labour'd up the sky.

Pope's precepts, in *An Essay on Criticism*, are better than his practice.

are none that should offer an English-speaker the slightest difficulty. Nor are they assembled into unorthodox syllabic patterns; every syllable in both lines conforms to the canonical pattern for English syllables.

A more advanced analysis might focus on a possible excess of consonant clusters and 'complex nuclei' ('long vowels', that is, a vowel plus a 'y' or 'w' glide), as a source for a sense of excess work done, or anticipated mentally, in pronunciation. It is possible that some lines of poetry might derive some of their stylistic effects from such a source, as, for example, Ben Jonson's line: 'Slow, slow, fresh fount, keep time with my salt tears.' In this line every syllable (with the exception of 'with') contains either a consonant cluster, or a complex nucleus; 'slow', 'fount', and 'tears' contain both. Yet even this line derives its major obstructive effects from other sources; its intonational obstructions are based, finally, on syntactic complexity.

In the Ajax lines of Pope, there are indeed syllables that contain either double or triple consonant clusters or complex nuclei, or both: the two syllables of 'Ajax' (however pronounced), 'strives', 'Rock's', 'vast', 'Weight', 'throw', 'Line', 'too', both syllables of 'labours', 'and', 'Words', 'move', 'slow'. This makes a total of fifteen out of twenty syllables, or almost as high an average as the Ben Jonson lines. It is also higher than the average for Pope's 'neutral' lines, as, for example, in lines 1–91 of *An Essay*, where an average line contains no more than two or three consonant clusters and three complex nuclei. The Ajax lines contain from four to six consonant clusters each, and five or six complex nuclei. Therefore it is possible to say, at least tentatively, that some of the sense of obstruction derives from an excess of phonic material to be articulated.

Much more obstructive, however, is the difficulty of transition from one syllable to the next in the first Ajax line. In three places – 'Ajax-strives', 'strives-some', 'weight-to' – the same or similar sounds end one syllable and begin the next. Normally (that is, in casual discourse), there would be no problem; the first of the similar sounds would be omitted, by a variety of elision. So, if the first Ajax line were a line from casual conversation, it might sound something like, 'When Ajak' strive' some Rock's vast Weigh' to throw.'

It is proof of the existence and the power of the 'formal style' of poetry reading, even in silent reading, that this elision does not operate here. Elision of this sort is not part of the way to perform in formal style, which is why Joos refers to a 'clattering' explicitness of pronunciation in his description. To pronounce both of the transitional border consonants, as in 'Ajax-strives', without elision requires a pause, an actual 'cessation of phonation'. This cessation, occurring three times in a short line, provides a major source for the feeling of obstruction: Ajax/strives, strives/some, weight/to. It is also proof of the operation of some other mode of performance than that of casual speech in the presence of poetry, one that Pope relies upon for part of his imitative effect, and with success: ten generations of readers have felt this obstruction. The cancellation of this elision in formal style seems to be the effect of a reader's socially inherited competence in the reading of poetry, and is therefore a 'normal' or, in this context, 'public' performance of a special sort of discourse.

Pope employs this technique with even more boldness in another 'representative' line from this section:

And ten low Words oft creep in one dull line.

(l. 347)

Here there is cancellation of elision, of one degree or another, in six places: and-ten, ten-low, low-Words, oft-creep, one-dull, dull-line. 'Ten-low' and 'one-dull' exhibit a cancellation of a lesser degree of elision, since the pairs /n/ and /l/, and /n/ and /d/, though not the same sounds, are too close in point of articulation (the tongue behind the teeth) to be pronounced in a formal style without a cessation of phonation, almost as if they were in danger of suffering elision. In a related phenomenon, the transitions 'words-oft' and 'creep-in' are too 'easy' for formal style; without a cessation of phonation, the pairs could sound like 'word-zoft' and 'cree-pin'. In this line, therefore, Pope deliberately sows difficulties in *every* transition, which is one of the reasons it is so 'dull', that is, 'obstructed'.

However, the main sources for the effect of obstruction in the Ajax lines are not to be found in the individual sounds, or their clustering, or their transition as such; they derive from intonational difficulties, articulations of a pattern which extends over larger stretches of the discourse than the sound, the syllable, or the syllable boundary. The second Ajax line, 'The Line too labours, and the Words move slow', is unlike the first in that it exhibits no transitional problems at all, and yet it seems *more* difficult to say than the first.

Two types of intonational description are required to describe these lines adequately enough so that the major sources of their obstruction can be clearly discerned: syllable-stress, and pitch and junctural patterning.[5]

1.
Stress

Every syllable in English has as its core a vowel (simple or complex); each syllable is characterized by a prominence, a special effort of articulation, generally centring on its vowel, which has been interpreted as a 'stress'. Exactly what stress is is still the subject of debate, as is the question of the number of the 'degrees' of stress, and whether these degrees have any absolute value. However, it is obvious that in English some syllables seem to be pronounced with more force than others. In most lines of poetry the pattern of stressed and unstressed syllables is clear: 'When *A*jax *strives, some Rock's vast Weight* to *throw*' ('some' should perhaps be unstressed, or less stressed). There is a pattern in stressing; only words from certain syntactic classes are entitled to a stress prominence: nouns, most verbs (not *to be* or *to become*, or other 'equational' verbs), adjectives (as *strictly* defined – not words like 'very' or 'the'), adverbs and adverbials, and some others. This assignment of stress in English according to word class seems to be based upon the information structure of the discourse; the words bearing the highest degree of new information also bear the highest stress. When new information becomes old information in a discourse, the stress is lost, as in pronouns: *John left*, but he *came back*. 'He' has no stress prominence here because it bears no new information.

Other syllables that have little stress prominence are those in polysyllabic words, unless these words are made up of shorter content-words; '*op*erator' and '*el*evator' each have a major stress, and three minor or missing ones, but when the two nouns are put together into '*el*evator-operator' the second element seems to lose its initial strong stress, perhaps because 'elevator-operator' is now *one* noun and is entitled to only one major stress. What had been the major stress on 'operator' is now reduced to something less than a major stress but more than no stress at all. The same situation applies to an adjective/noun combination; when 'the *bird* is *black*' is pronounced, both 'bird' and 'black', as information words, are entitled to major stresses. However, in the phrase 'the *black bird*', the stress on 'black' seems to be less than in 'the bird is black', though it still seems to be 'major', i.e. stronger than the stress on 'the'.[6]

So, to judge by ear (or, perhaps, by expectation plus ear), there seem to be major stresses, and minor stresses, and some sort of intermediate stresses. Although the traditional metrical treatment of stress in English only distinguishes strong from weak, just how many degrees of stress there are, and how they are assigned, is still very much of a problem. Early investigators like Sweet suggest that there are three

stress levels; later linguists such as Trager and Smith postu-
late four. Chomsky and Halle, while denying that degrees
of stress are always physically present in utterances, nevertheless suggest up to five degrees of stress, assignable ultimately on the basis of the syntax of the utterance. Philip
Lieberman reports experiments which seem to show that
although some degrees of stress *were* discernible by different
hearers, the number of degrees varied from two to five, with
very little agreement about the assignment of grades of stress
between the extremes; that is, degrees of stress between the
highest and lowest were randomly distributed by those
tested. [7] Again, these results may be affected by the notorious
'looseness' of normal enunciation in casual discourse (the
phenomenon that produces elision discussed above), which
may not be so loose in the performance of poetry, or of discourse in the 'formal style'.

The 'minimal' stress system that discerns only two levels
of stress, strong and weak, seems inadequate to describe the
Ajax lines. [8] Here, some of the spondees can be explained by
the excessive number of short information words. 'Vast
Weight' and 'move slow', two of the possible four spondees
in two lines, are spondees because of the immediate juxta-
position of two monosyllabic words of that kind. The other
spondee, 'too, la[bours]', and the possible fourth spondee,
'some Rock's', cannot be so explained, however; 'too' and
'some' are not information words. On the other hand, 'too' is
a 'transition marker' or sequence marker, a sort of marshal
of the discourse, keeping the sentences in order, and transition markers like 'too', 'first', 'then', and so on, also bear a
major stress. That is one reason why 'too, la[bours]' is a
spondee.

The case of 'some Rock's' is more difficult. 'Some' is not
an information word; syntactically it seems to be either a
determiner like 'the' or 'a', or a numeral, like 'three', but,
unlike 'three', indefinite in number. 'The' or 'a' never bear
major stresses (except in contrastive situations, as in 'You're

not *the* John Jones'); numerals, as a special (rather odd) class of adjectives bear an intermediate degree of stress. However, 'some' in 'some Rock's' is *not* an indefinite numeral, since we know how many rocks Ajax will be throwing (one); what we do not know is *which* rock he will throw. Consequently, it is doubtful whether 'some Rock's' is a spondee, or merely a heavy type of iamb. ('Some' as in 'some Rock's' has been called an 'indefinite demonstrative', and demonstratives do not bear major stress, unless they emphasize a contrast '*these* men, not *those*'.)

It seems to be necessary for the description of the rhythm of poetry (its *actual* intonation, as distinguished from its metre) to be able to assign intermediate degrees of stress. Otherwise every iambic pentameter line would be analysed like every other, with insertions of spondees and pyrrhic feet perhaps for the doubtful cases. What metrists have been describing as 'hovering feet' or, as Vladimir Nabokov calls it, 'scud',[9] are those in which the syllables contrast weakly with each other, sometimes because they display some variety of intermediate stress. In the Ajax lines, the spondees and the pyrrhic feet all seem to be of different weights.

(*a*) 'some Rock's' is a doubtful spondee. If a major stress were numbered 1 and no-stress numbered 4, the pattern for this foot would, it seems to me, be something like 'some Rock's', for a very low degree of contrast, but with some contrast in a weaker/stronger pattern – in other words, a type of iamb.

(*b*) 'vast Weight' is much heavier, but even here, to my subjective ear, it is not really a spondee. I would assign a 2–1 pattern to it ('vast Weight'), again as a type of iamb, if an odd one.

(*c*) 'too, la[bours]' is close to a 'true' spondee, 'too, la', complicated, however, by the pitch pattern (to be described below).

(d) '-bours, and' – this foot (the pyrrhic foot) is, sub-
jectively again, quite weak in stress; but, while
assigning no more than a 4–4 pattern to it (the
weakest possible), the *actual material* pronounced in
'-bours' requires more effort than 'and'. It is doubtful,
however, if we should mix systems this way in the
determination of the inherent rhythm of a line. Perhaps a measure of syllable *weight* could provide a
parallel measure to the line's inherent *stress* rhythm.

(e) 'move slow': for reasons to be treated below, this foot
is a very heavy spondee indeed: perhaps 'móve slów'
like 'tóo, là-', and for essentially the same reason. The
rise in pitch on 'slow' may suggest that 'slow' has a
heavier stress than 'move', but this may be an illusion.
Indeed, the relationship between stress and pitch is
highly complex and has not yet been satisfactorily
described.

Therefore, of the four spondees in the Ajax lines, two are
heavy spondees ('tóo, là', and 'móve slów'), one is weaker and
more iambic ('vàst Wéight') and one is very much weaker
('sòme Ròck's') and may not be spondaic at all. What all
these feet have in common is a contiguity of stress and
weight – in none of them is the first syllable more than one
degree weaker than the second. A 'true' iamb, it would seem,
must be truly contrastive; it must display patterns like 3–1,
4–1, or 4–2. Anything closer begins to break the iambic
metre, a fragile flower at best.

2. Pitch and juncture

But the obstructive effect in the Ajax lines derives as much if
not more from pitch and junctural phenomena as from
transition difficulties or stress heaviness.

Stress, pitch and juncture as stylistic phenomena in

English can be omitted without losing the meaning of an utterance, if, in casual discourse, the speaker performs in a gabbling monotone. For most utterances which are unambiguous syntactically, pitch and juncture are not strictly necessary for communication: the *facta*, or *what*, that is involved, may be adequately communicated with out them. For example, internal juncture (which can here be described as a kind of internal pause) can be omitted, or be minimally present, or maximally present, without much effect on the meaning of the line 'John loves Mary'.

(*a*) None: John-loves-Mary
(*b*) Minimal: John | loves-Mary
(*c*) Maximal: John | loves | Mary

In (*a*) there is no internal pause; in (*b*) there is one; and in (*c*) there are two. All three performances are equally acceptable in terms of the communication of information.

However, this is not to say that omission of juncture is entirely without penalty, and here we clearly enter the sphere of *stilus*, of *how*, in respect of the information that is communicated (see pp. 22–4 above). In this sphere, *external* juncture (between sentences) seems to be less expendable than *internal* juncture; when someone says, all in one breath,

John-loves-Mary-I-hate-them-both

there is an impression of haste and incomplete control of emotion. This is not necessarily so if the speaker produces an external juncture but no internal ones for the utterance:

John-loves-Mary | I-hate-them-both

In addition, if there *is* internal juncture, it must also follow certain rules of precedence, or a spasmodic, hesitant effect is produced. In

John-loves | Mary

it sounds as if the speaker wished to produce a dramatic effect by delaying the name of Mary, or could not bring himself to say it. Of course, if there is an internal juncture (even a correct one) and no external one, the effect is even odder:

John | loves-Mary-I-hate-them-both

While there is nothing to prevent speakers from gabbling, or jerking out their sentences spasmodically, the very fact that their performance can be described by such pejoratives as 'gabbling' or 'spasmodic' suggests that there are regular traditional or canonical styles of performing sentences and discourse, or of expecting them to be performed.

With this system in mind for most normal utterances, let us examine 'abnormal' ones. Inversion of normal sentence order produces what we might call 'emergency phonology'. In such situations, internal junctures and odd pitch patterns multiply. For example, the pitch-juncture pattern of a normal sentence – 'the three boys drank beer in the café' – could be

the-three-boys | drank-beer | in-the-café.

Inverted – 'the three boys drank, in the café, beer' – will probably sound like:

the-three-boys | drank | in-the-café | beer.

The internal junctures are much more necessary in the inverted situation, and there are more of them. In addition, unusual syntactic structures are signalled by the odd pitch-curlicues and pauses indicating a noticeable oddity in style.

Pope employs this scheme in his poetic game. In the first Ajax line, the inversion of 'some Rock's vast Weight' introduces intonation complexities, enjoining the use of three internal junctures instead of two.

Normal order: When Ajax | strives | to throw some Rock's vast Weight

Inverted: When Ajax | strives | some Rock's vast
              Weight | to throw

There is another reason, a very interesting one, for the
obstruction in this line. 'Some Rock's vast Weight' is not a
literal expression; since he throws an attribute of the rock,
not the rock itself, it is a 'metonymy of adjunct'. I feel that
there is a convention (a 'paralinguistic'[10] convention)
covering the style of such non-literal stretches of utterance
as those containing distinctive rhetorical figures of this sort:
the speaker slows down the tempo of the utterance (or
imagines it slowing) to signal the secondary interpretive
nature of the rhetoric. To test this notion, imagine that 'some
Rock' were changed to 'Sum Rok', and it were regarded as
the name of a Korean wrestler. Then the phrase 'Sum Rok's
vast weight' would have a literal though bizarre meaning;
Ajax would be described as attempting to throw an enormous piece of equipment owned by a Korean wrestler, and
there would be no slowing of tempo:

When Ajax strives *some Rock's vast Weight* to throw
            [slowing of tempo]
When Ajax strives *Sum Rok's vast weight* to throw
            [no slowing of tempo]

Therefore, by a combination of transition difficulties, a
certain excess of information words with a concomitant
increase in major stresses, emergency phonology (for the
inversion) and paralinguistic slowing of tempo (for the
rhetorical figure), Pope achieves a very obstructed and difficult style of performance in the first Ajax line.

This obstruction is relevant to the content of the line and
reinforces it; the sound (actual or potential) seems 'an
echo to the sense'. However, if the sense were entirely different, or opposite, but the phonological and paralinguistic
reasons for obstruction remained, an obstructive performance would still be inevitable, but it would not now seem to

reflect the content. As in Robert Browning, for example, it might seem to be characteristic of the personal style of the poet, and not part of the public literature game: 'When Ajax strives some toy's light weight to toss' is as difficult to perform as the original, but the obstruction now has a different function, and perhaps indicates a hesitant or awkward style in the speaker.

In the second Ajax line, the obstruction is not due to transition problems at all, nor are there any noticeable rhetorical figures to slow the tempo. In

The Line too *labours*, and the Words move *slow*

there is no difficulty in moving from syllable to syllable. However, there is an inversion, with concomitant 'emergency phonology', though of rather a different sort than in the first line.

The performance of

$$\overline{\text{The Line labours}\,|\,\text{too}}$$

is much easier than

$$\overline{\text{The Line}\,|\,\text{too}\,|\,\text{labours}}$$

There is, however, a much more subtle source for the obstruction than syntactic inversion in this half-line. The use of 'too' is mildly unorthodox, as we will see, and the nature of this difficulty causes a difficulty in the speaker's forming a hypothesis about the syntactic structure of the line, and therefore a difficulty in being able to 'perform' the line.

Any line which is syntactically ambiguous will be difficult to perform. 'We move on Tuesday' could be performed as

(*a*) We-move | on-Tuesday
(*b*) We-move-on | Tuesday

with concomitant differences in meaning based on different syntactic structures. The speaker, confronted by the (written) sentence 'We move on Tuesday', might hesitate before he launches out on a performance, or perhaps perform it in a mechanically divided manner:

We | move | on | Tuesday.

This bears out Chomsky's contention that ungrammatical 'strings', sequences of words to which it is difficult or impossible to assign a syntax, tend to be performed as strings of unrelated words.[11]

This condition applies to the first half-line of the second Ajax line. 'The Line too *labours*' is semi-grammatical because of an unorthodox use of 'too', and this semi-grammaticality brings about a potential hesitation in performance. The sentence does not fall apart into a string of unrelated words – it is not *un*grammatical – but it is not immediately perceivable as transparently grammatical and performable as such.

The orthodox rule governing the use of 'too' (not the intensifier 'too' of course, as in 'too hot') is clear and unequivocal:

Too is to be used only as an indicator
of repetition, and only in a sentence differing
from the *too*-sentence in *one* particular.

The orthodox operation of *too* can be seen in

John likes music.
John likes art, too.*

It would sound very odd to go violently against the rule:

?? John likes music.
?? Mary likes beer, too.

---

* Note, however, that in other contexts, 'proforms' like 'do' and 'so' may be present without altering the operation of the rule:
John likes music.
Mary does, too (=Mary likes music, too).

This rule is so rigid that when it is infringed even slightly there is a hesitation in accepting the result:

John likes Botticelli.
? Mary likes art, too.

The single question mark suggests that while the rule is ultimately seen to be followed, there is a lack of 'transparency', and a consequent hesitation in processing the result. In short, there is semi-grammaticality.

This is the situation in the Ajax lines.

When Ajax strives . . .
The Line too labours.

'Strives' and 'labours' are closely synonymous, but they are *not the same word*, and the hesitation concomitant with this situation causes a hesitation in performing the line, and thus determines its 'hesitant' style. The hesitation would not exist if 'labours' were replaced by 'strives', as the reader can experience by pronouncing them:

When Ajax strives . . .
The Line too strives . . .

The internal junctures in

The Line | too | labours

are thereby lengthened by the hesitation. It seems to me that the pitch pattern also is altered, becoming higher than normal over 'too', possibly as a result of the performance of a semi-grammatical utterance.

Semi-grammaticality of an even subtler cast accounts for the obstruction in the second half-line, 'and the Words move slow'. The line would move more quickly, that is, with fewer internal junctures, if it were one syllable longer! If 'slow' were 'slowly' the performance would not include an internal pause that is otherwise potentially there:

The-Words | move | slow
The-Words | move-slowly

The presence of the adjective form 'slow' for the more regular adverb form 'slowly' produces a semi-grammaticality. The adjective-form is not *un*grammatical; there is ample precedent for such a construction in such phrases as:

> The candle burned blue.
> Charles jumped clear [of the ship].
> The moon shines bright.

However, this 'quasi-predicative' form, as it has been termed,[12] is not as regular in English as the common *verb manner-adverb* construction ('the candle burned brightly'), and this semi-grammaticality also causes hesitation.*

The second Ajax line, therefore, owes its sense of obstruction *entirely* to the performer's hesitation in deciding what the syntax is of each half-line, and whether the half-line in question is truly grammatical. Except for the emergency phonology attendant upon the inversion of 'too', the style of the line is entirely a matter of high-level mental processing, and has nothing to do with the sort of low-level phonological-articulatory processing that accounts for the obstruction of the first Ajax line.

In playing the public literature game, Pope has so deftly built a wide range of stylistic obstructions into the Ajax lines that he has managed to manipulate the reading habits of his audience long after his own death. The public literature game has rarely been played so brilliantly – or so openly.

This sort of analysis has two results. First, it enables the critic to be completely precise about the source of stylistic effects. Second, and consequently, the craft of a master poet becomes accessible, not only to critics, but to other

---

* Perhaps some other word than 'semi-grammaticality' should be used here, since one form is as 'grammatical' as the other. The difference seems to be one of statistically preponderant choice – if this can be established, perhaps 'crypto-grammatical' would be better. The resultant hesitation in performance, however, is the same.

poets. If a poet wished to write an obstructed line, or to re-
move obstruction from a line, this sort of analysis could help
him. For example, it should be possible by such a technique to write a line that was so obstructed that it would be
very difficult indeed to perform. I suggest that the following
line (which I have just composed) provides an example of
egregious obstruction:

Ring-grim, my great Tom-cat, nears slow
winter's swamp

If the reader will give this line a careful performance, it
should read very slowly and with difficulty. The doubt about
whether 'slow' modifies 'winter' or not seems to me to reinforce the hesitation past the point of semi-grammaticality,
and the transitional difficulties are almost insuperable.

The public game III: syntax

As we have seen above, the intonation of a line of poetry is,
like the intonation of every other sort of utterance, con-
siderably determined by its syntax. However, the syntax of a
line of poetry, or a complete poem, may be shaped by the
poet for other purposes than those of intonation.

In a poem by Robert Lowell[13] (which is about, among
other things, pollution of the environment) there is a powerful line:

There sewage sickens the rebellious seas.

Much of the vigour of the line derives from what seems to be
a fight over precedence between the verb and the adjective: just how permanent is the 'rebellion', and what is
the temporal relationship between the rebelling and the
sickening? The reader is required to mediate among the
following possible meanings:

(*a*) Sewage sickens the seas, which once had been

rebellious but because of pollution are now too 'sickened' to resist further pollution.

(b) Sewage sickens the seas which once had been rebellious against pollution, but although still rebellious are rapidly losing the will to rebel.

(c) Sewage sickens the seas, which, however sickened, are still, and will continue to be, rebellious when faced with a threat of pollution.

(d) The seas have been and always will be rebellious, whether or not they are threatened with pollution, but their natural and external rebellion is presently contending with a sickening power – pollution.

(e) Sewage sickens the seas, which become rebellious upon sensing the encroachment of pollution.

Syntactic structures account for the various interpretations as well as the total effect of conflict caused by the fight of interpretations. The effects turns upon the position of 'rebellious'. There are two possible positions for noun-modifiers in English:

(a) after the noun, as complete relative clauses ('the hat *which was black*') or reduced ('the man *dancing on the table*');

(b) before the noun, as simple or complex noun-modifiers ('the *black* hat')

Noun-modifiers before the noun suggest permanent qualities of the noun they modify: compare 'the man dancing' with 'the dancing man'.[14] The seas are *permanently* rebellious, since the modifier is *before* the noun; how can they be sickened? Yet permanent rebellion is difficult to imagine; usually it follows upon provocation. Hence the reader's hesitation and conflict, and his search for ways out of the contradiction – all useful for the poet's purpose. We have here what would otherwise be thought of as an inefficiency of expression – an ambiguity – used for dramatic purposes.

This oddity of noun-modification resembles the so-called 'proleptic' modifier, as in: 'In the midst of a peaceful scene, the sultan suddenly shouted at his *terrified* wives.' 'Terrified' is 'proleptic', or anticipatory since the wives are terrified only as a *result* of the shouting. A non-proleptic version of the line would be: 'In the midst of a peaceful scene, the sultan suddenly shouted, and terrified his wives.' The proleptic modifier is a well-known device of Greek and Latin rhetoric, and its effect depends entirely upon the usual interpretation of noun-modifiers, which express a condition existing *simultaneously* with that expressed by the verb, or at least not affected by it. If the modifier is proleptic this simultaneity cannot exist for semantic reasons, and a heterodox sequential interpretation is enforced upon the line.

Only one of the five interpretations of the Lowell line is truly proleptic – that given in (*e*). The others also involve an unorthodox sequence but are not entirely anticipatory. Some could, in fact, be called 'anaproleptic' (but not 'epileptic'!), in that the rebelliousness may not be entirely or at all the *result* of the sickening.

Notice also that the problem could almost vanish if the sentence were in the passive:

The rebellious seas are sickened by sewage.

In the passive form the rebellion *precedes* the sickening in the sentence form, and therefore makes much less likely any interpretations (like (*c*) or (*d*)) which suggest a possibility of continued resistance. Lowell, however, provides an active sentence, with the order of the sickening and the rebellion in doubt, a sentence whose style thus mimes the intensity of the conflict.

Lowell's creative use of conflict between an active verb ('sicken') and a permanent (or semi-permanent) quality expressed by the noun-modifier ('rebellious') was anticipated by Blake. In *Vala*, Blake writes of

... cities, turrets & towers & domes
  Whose smoke destroy'd the pleasant gardens, & whose
    running kennels
  Chok'd the bright rivers.

Here the permanence of 'pleasant' and 'bright' are cast in doubt, since it is just these qualities which are 'destroy'd' and 'chok'd'; the subsequent conflict of interpretation closely resembles that of the Lowell lines. In Blake's poem, the adjectives are, in fact, 'anaproleptic', in that they represent conditions which have already been altered by the verb.

It could be said that Blake (and Lowell) have simply made syntactical errors which seem here to contribute little if anything to the poetry of the lines, if it were not for Blake's astonishing affirmation of his 'error' in *Jerusalem*. In the first stanza, England's mountains are 'green' and her pastures 'pleasant'. These are 'true' adjectives representing permanent qualities, the reader assumes (even though they are placed after the noun in an archaic fashion). Yet as the poem progresses the dark Satanic mills press around the speaker; what now of the 'permanent' green and pleasantness of England? Nevertheless, in the last stanza, Blake's syntax deliberately repeats his attribution of 'green and pleasant', as if to reiterate a basic conviction that, however the surface may appear, these remain the permanent, visionary and unalterable qualities of England's land.

A good deal of research into many aspects of the relationship between style and syntax has been undertaken in recent years. The present writer has examined syntactic patterning in Hopkins and Blake; M. A. K. Halliday and the present writer have examined Yeats's use of syntax to establish a mood of timelessness; Marjorie Perloff has performed suggestive syntactic analyses on the poetry of Robert Lowell, demonstrating syntactic rhythms miming cognitive patterns; Donald Freeman has been working on the use of syntax by Keats, Blake, and Dylan Thomas; Seymour Chatman, in addition to other projects, has shown how Milton's use of passive noun-modifiers ('the *created* world') in *Paradise Lost* suggests the presence of the Creator in the world without actually mentioning Him; Irene Fairley has worked extensively on e e cummings; and S. J. Keyser has analysed Wallace Stevens's use of syntactic parallelism and tenses, and the methods by which Stevens forces the reader to re-evaluate the syntax of the poem as he goes along, thus miming its essential thematic elements. These are by no means all of the critics working in this rich new field. The American critic Stanley Fish has been providing a critical underpinning for the analysis of a reader's (putative) reaction to language elements as formal structures in literature, for an 'affective stylistics'. Roman Jakobson, as the originator of this school, has constantly provided both theory and precept.[15]

Modern poets experiment ceaselessly with syntax, for their special effects. Yeats abruptly begins the poem *The Cold Heaven*, from his early-middle period, with the line:

Suddenly I saw the cold and rook-delighting heaven

'Suddenly' is a sequence marker whose use is normally justified only as an evidence of an abrupt transition from a first state to a second. Yeats provides no first state, so the reader is thrust abruptly into the discourse, far too abruptly, as we shall see, for the syntactically complex material he is being asked to absorb. Once into the discourse, the reader is 'suddenly' required to interpret an unorthodox syntax in the object of the sentence. The modifiers of 'heaven' are not restrictive; that is, Yeats is not making a distinction between a cold and rook-delighting heaven and some other kind. A non-restrictive modifier always carries an emotive charge, perhaps because it is 'by-the-way'; it always bears gratuitous information, information not seen to be necessary to describe a situation, and thereby valued only for itself.

Restrictive	*Non-restrictive*
I saw *two* girls.	I saw a girl.
The blonde girl winked.	The blonde girl winked.
(= the girl who was blonde winked)	(= the girl, who, by the way, was blonde, winked)

In the 'restrictive' situation, the memory of blondness occurs during the cognitive action underlying and producing the first sentence, perhaps as part of the recognition of the two girls, or just afterwards. It emerges as the restrictive modifier 'blonde' in the second sentence, as an essential distinguisher of the two. There is no emotion attached to it and its function as a distinguisher is entirely utilitarian (although perhaps the 'blondness' does have more value for the observer than would any other possible distinguisher). In the 'non-restrictive' situation, however, it is almost as if the memory of the blondness occurred as the second sentence was beginning to be created or uttered. The value of the blondness was suddenly so extreme that the speaker could not wait to create a separate sentence – 'By the way, the girl was blond' – since it was too urgent to put off. A cognitive diagram for the creation of the sentences might look like this:

Restrictive

Actual speech : I saw two girls. The blonde girl winked.
Cognitive : (notices two girls: one blonde) (notices winking)

Non-restrictive

Actual speech : I saw a girl. The blonde girl winked.
Cognitive : (notices a girl) (notices winking) (notices blondness)

Observe that there seems to be a contrapuntal structure in the non-restrictive situation, with the 'winking' creating a sentence, only to have the 'blondness' forcing itself into it when it is only half-created. If the blondness were less startling or valuable to the observer (if it were to wait its turn), the patterns would probably be:

Actual speech:	I saw a girl.	The girl winked.
	By the way, the girl was blonde.	
Cognitive:	(notices a girl)	(notices winking)
	(notices blondness)	

This sequence of three sentences would mirror a casual and consecutive rhythm of cognition, with observations strung out like beads on a thread, with nothing so valuable that you cannot wait to describe it.

In the line, 'Suddenly I saw the cold and rook-delighting heaven', the double modifiers of 'heaven' – 'cold' and 'rook-delighting' – seem so intensely important that even when the mind of the speaker, 'suddenly' thrust into speech, is beginning to express his vision of heaven, *both* the coldness of heaven *and* its capacity to delight rooks, forces itself upon him and into his half-formed locution. A single non-restrictive modifier, as in the blonde-girl example above, shows the mind operating contrapuntally, at a greater tempo than usual. If, as in *The Cold Heaven*, there are *two* non-restrictive modifiers intruding at a time when the mind is working at full stretch anyway ('suddenly'), the mind of the speaker must be at a supernatural pitch, racing like the wind of heaven itself. Indeed, Yeats has many poems in which he represents his mind, proceeding in its quotidian rhythm, being suddenly assaulted by eternity; *The Cold Heaven* is one of the earliest and best.

This sort of analysis, the description of the varying rhythms and overlays of cognition which produce various syntactic patternings, provides a clear and vivid method of showing the operation of the mind in the double contrapuntal act of observing and expressing. With the revelation of the value system of the speaker – what he values too highly to postpone expressing – this aspect of the public literature game comes close to the other concern of stylistic analysis, the revelation of private individual personality. It is with this subtle and complex technique that we come to the borders of the public game and begin to cross over into the private one.

4 THE PRIVATE GAME: PORTRAITS OF THE ARTIST

THE 'individuality' of individual persons is something we all recognize. We can recognize our friends, and distinguish them from 'just anybody'. Perhaps we can even recognize ourselves. By the operation of the schema of style outlined above, we can first distinguish objective phenomena, recorded as sensory data, and identify them as distinctively human ways of behaving. This is already a stylistic distinction. We can then proceed to a further step, the particular 'way of being human' characteristic of our old friend Charlie, for instance, and no one else. Charlie is distinguished from just anybody by perceived stylistic differences. The bundle of phenomena we call Charlie differs from any other identified bundle, if only in terms of space and time: no other person can occupy the same space at the same time as someone else; so even if almost all the sensory signals were the same for two individuals, they would still be distinguished stylistically as two (and not one) by position in space and time.

This subject is filled with paradoxes and difficulties, and in this part of the book, the particular stylistic distinctiveness of the individual will be treated in general and tentative terms.

Many more questions will be asked than answered. We will concentrate on the stylistic distinctiveness of literary artists, as exemplified by their use of language.

The uses of language in the public games already described are not characteristic, as such, of the poets employing them, but rather seem to be evoked by the specific occasions of the poems in which they are employed. The ability of the poet to rise to the occasion is not an individualizing trait of the artist but a general ability of the poet as craftsman in the public literature game. When Pope makes the reader hesitate in performing the Ajax lines from *An Essay on Criticism*, when Hopkins and Yeats cause a subjective rise in spirits in the reader by programming a buccal lift, and when Donne performs the opposite feat in 'a bracelet of bright hair about the bone', these effects characterize the public skill of accomplished artists; they are not distinguishing signs of the style of these writers as individuals. We must look elsewhere for the portrait of the artist, and the effect of the stamp of specific individuality on the reader of a literary artefact.

It has long been the practice of literary critics, especially Continental ones in the Romantic tradition, to attempt to isolate the private characteristics or personal philosophies of writers, as distinguished in their language styles. Leo Spitzer discerns in Cervantes a characteristic avoidance of commitment in relation to proper names in *Don Quixote*; the Don himself has three versions of his family name, as well as a number of periphrastic titles. Other characters in the novel are treated with the same consistent lack of definition, which Spitzer suggests is a private characteristic of Cervantes himself. In the works of Diderot, on the other hand, the characteristic clue to the personality of the author is not on such a semiotically complex level, but rather consists of syntactic rhythms reminiscent of those of such bodily functions as sexual intercourse. In the work of the novelist Charles-Louis Philippe, Spitzer finds an excessive use of unjustified causatives, as if Philippe were attempting to explain connections that he himself was uneasily aware were not there.[1]

The tradition of distinguishing personality traits in the characteristic use of language by writers is Continental in origin. However, critics in the Anglo-American tradition have recently been active in the same pursuit. One of the most impressive analyses in this field has been performed by Anthony Burgess on the chameleon of style himself, James Joyce. While admitting that Joyce has indeed a formidable array of other people's styles at his command, Burgess will not therefore admit that personal style is henceforth redundant, and that only collage techniques remain. Joyce *has* a style, a paradoxically 'impersonal' but distinctive approach to 'what might be termed literary engineering'. Burgess quotes a number of sentences from *Ulysses*:

(*a*) The bungholes sprang open and a huge dull flood leaked out, flowing together, winding through mudflats all over the level land, a lazy pooling swirl of liquor bearing along wideleaved flowers of its froth.

(*b*) The cold smell of sacred stone called him.

(*c*) He waited by the counter, inhaling the keen reek of drugs, the dusty dry smell of sponges and loofahs.

(*d*) He foresaw his pale body reclined in it at full, naked, in a womb of warmth, oiled by scented melting soap, softly laved.

Burgess argues that the reader's vocal equipment is thoroughly exercised by Joyce's writing: 'each sentence seems to play a tune independent of the sense. It is as if Joyce were given a keyboard capable of striking all the English vowel phonemes and he at once began to play as many different ones as he could, leaping in wide intervals rather than treading a scale.' He also finds in these sentences 'language behaving a fraction more unexpectedly than we would find' in an ordinary novelist. The language contains 'small lexical surprises' – the coldness of the sacred stone, the keen reek of the drugs. Burgess believes that 'there is a curiously impersonal quality' about Joyce's playing of the linguistic instrument; 'it is the impersonality, of course, that Joyce requires'.[2]

However, this 'impersonality' is not what it seems. Joyce, in fact, deploys three styles, all 'impersonal' in one way or another, but all these cohere to produce a portrait of the artist. In addition to Joyce's notorious skill in borrowing the styles of others, and the 'impersonal' style discerned by Burgess, there is a third style, even more 'impersonal' in intention than the other two, which attempts to secure the *phrase juste*, in the Flaubertian tradition. Here, the notion of style as private idiosyncratic personal choice, based on personal intellectual 'rhythms', is swallowed up in the task of discovering the *only* public way to express some external or internal process, one, in theory, not affected by personal idiosyncrasies.[3]

Joyce often succeeds in being directly imitative in this third manner, and therefore truly impersonal. In the famous last line from the Proteus chapter, he mimes the mental process which first perceives attributes, and then combines them to form a noun:

> Moving through the air high spars of a threemaster, her sails brailed up on the crosstrees, homing, upstream, silently moving, a silent ship.[4]

The mind first perceives a motion in the air, then notices the three masts (though without yet arriving at the word 'ship'), then notices the sails, and identifies the destination of the motion, observes the silence of the approach, and finally, summing up all of the attributes, arrives at the word 'ship'. However buccally active the sentence is, it escapes being classified as 'characteristically Joycean' through its attempt to express the only and thus inevitable way to describe the experience exactly. This is not Joyce's 'personal' style, that of playing on an 'impersonal' instrument; this is Joyce (and humanity with him) publicly discovering the *only* way to describe the approach of such a ship. Joyce's three styles – pastiche, Burgessian virtuosity, Flaubertian mimesis – are not 'personal' in the traditional Romantic sense, but they do characterize the modern creator in the Romantic line.

There have been a number of recent treatments of this kind, of writers' individual traits – Milic on Swift, Paul Kiparsky on Walt Whitman, Ohmann on Matthew Arnold and Shaw, among many others.[5] Richard Ohmann speaks for this school of criticism with his declaration that 'literary criticism is the study of mental structures'. The structures in the text as perceived by the reader can indicate distinctive choices of diction and syntax, or more high-level structures of content and of rhetorical approach. These structures outline the 'epistemic choices' or the path taken by the thinking process, and suggest the shape of the writer's mind and of his individual style:

> The very many decisions that add up to a style are decisions about what to say, as well as how to say it. They reflect the writer's organization of experience, his sense of life, so that the most general of his attitudes and ideas find expression just as characteristically in his style as in his matter, though less overtly. Style, in this view, far from being intellectually peripheral ornament, is what I have called 'epistemic choice', and the study of style can lead to an insight into the writer's most confirmed epistemic stances.[6]

We have seen above how Ohmann discerns the hard-driving character of D. H. Lawrence in his characteristic repetition (with deletion) of sentences. Ohmann also finds characteristic effects in the syntax of Henry James, Faulkner, and Hemingway, effects depending upon choice between different syntaxes for the 'same' content.[7]

The resources of transformational-generative grammar are helpful here since, at one stage of the development of that science, 'optional' transformations were postulated: re-orderings of the elements of declarative sentences to produce strings of words whose import was generally 'the same' as that of the 'original' structure but whose appearance was different. Sentences like 'Bill was kicked by John', and 'It was John who kicked Bill' were held to be paraphrases of each other, and of sentences like 'John kicked Bill'. Different individuals would produce stylistically differing paraphrases of the same basic utterance.* This phenomenon has been noted independently by Orwell, in his description of the style of Big Brother:

> Winston thought for a moment, then pulled the speak-write toward him and began dictating in Big Brother's familiar style: a style at once military and pedantic, and, because of a trick of asking questions and then promptly answering them ('What lessons do we learn from this fact, comrades? The lessons – which is one of the fundamental principles of Ingsoc – that', etc., etc.), easy to imitate.[8]

Winston's ability to produce a pastiche of Big Brother's style testifies to the presence of 'epistemic choice' in Big Brother's syntax. The 'self-questioning' transformation, as it could be called, is immediately recognizable as a stylistic trait of the entity 'Big Brother'. This can be distinguished from a less characterizing type of utterance, which would be something like: 'Comrades, we learn lessons from the fact – lessons which [demonstrate] one of the fundamental

---

* 'John kicked Bill' was, at one stage of the development of Chomskyan syntax, regarded as somehow more basic (or 'simplex') than its paraphrases. The notion that the simplex utterance 'means the same' as its paraphrases has been under attack. Certainly the effect of 'It was John who kicked Bill' is different from that of 'John kicked Bill'. However, their truth values are the same: if 'John kicked Bill' is true, then its paraphrases are true and vice versa.

principles of Ingsoc, that . . .'; or perhaps a simpler discourse entirely: 'Comrades, we learn lessons from the fact. These lessons are that . . . This is one of the fundamental principles of Ingsoc.' These sentences can be recognized as paraphrases of Orwell's text but without the 'characteristic' self-questioning.

Even here we have a certain difficulty in regarding this insight as one which indicates a particular, distinctive personality. For one thing, Big Brother is almost certainly a composite, a name like Pharoah, or The O'Neill, the title of a leader, so the 'individuality' of his style is a false one, and easily imitated by those whose function it is to speak in his name. This uneasy blend of personality and synthetic structure is, in fact, characteristic of the society controlled by Big Brother in the novel, and reflects the psychological presuppositions of the rulers of that society – private personality is an abomination to them. Big Brother has a style which is made up of recognizable elements from military and academic backgrounds, the least talented but most common representatives of both. This problem, however, is a general problem with this sort of analysis: how much of the material analysed is personal style and how much is impersonal borrowings? And what 'personality' emerges?

The problem is compounded when the choice of words (*lexis*) of a writer, rather than his choice of syntax acts as the determining criterion of style. How can we tell which words he characteristically favours? How do we recognize a 'deviation' from general patterns of word choice? It is likely that the range of general choice of words cannot be defined explicitly. There are, to be sure, a few dozen words – functors – which appear with roughly the same frequency in the writings of almost everybody, words like 'the', 'of', 'in', 'to' and so on; a few hundred words account for more than 85 per cent of any text, and those remaining, which usually bear the content weight of any text, jostle non-significantly for the role of 'outstanding' words.[9] I have noticed, for example, that Orwell often uses 'disgusting' unexpectedly, in the middle of a context in which he is obviously trying to be neutral in tone, and to keep his temper. It is as if the underlying revulsion cannot be indefinitely kept under. This observation does not come from a careful statistical analysis of Orwell's style but rather from a Riffaterrian intuition of a departure from a norm, derived from the continuous unconscious process of analysis which takes place during the act of reading Orwell (see below, p. 75).

Joyce employs 'old' and its derivatives 612 times in *Ulysses*, which brings it out of the range of information words and well up within the range of common functors; it is actually more common than such words as 'this', 'are', 'we', 'which' and so on. 'Young' and its derivatives only appear 210 times. In *Finnegans Wake*, 'old' and its derivatives occur (undisguised) 535 times, which a rough check reveals to be more than any other word in the *Wake*, not counting the hundred most commonly appearing words; 'young' appears only 91 times. In Yeats's poetry, 'old' and its derivatives appear 575 times, which makes it the most common information word in his poetic work next to 'all' (if that is an information word). It may seem significant that the same word 'old' has such a statistical predominance in the works of both Irish writers; but the method employed to discover this is, as the reader can see from the above, nothing more than the following up of an intuition, employing only an inexplicit method of description, perhaps because no other method is justified.

The whole question takes on an unreal glow when we realize that we are attributing prominence to a word because it appears in a text fifty times, rather than forty — and this in a text where the most common words in the language each appear several hundred or even several thousand times! The notion of 'general' lexical prominence vanishes in a cloud of squabbles over insignificant precedences. What is it to the general structure of English if the word 'disgusting' appears a few more times than you might expect in the works of Orwell, or the word 'old' in the works of both Joyce and Yeats, or that Yeats uses derivatives of the word 'sudden' sixty-eight times in his poetry?[10] How many times does the average speaker of the language use these words, and is it really possible to set up elaborate tables of precedence and reach conclusions about style on the basis of such meagre representation? Except for the most commonly used words of the language, all tables of general usage merely reflect, with considerable accuracy, the content of the texts chosen for analysis, and little more.

Word choice may be, and indeed, very likely is, in the realm of personal choice and idiosyncrasy; Riffaterre[11] persuasively notes prominent appearances of certain words in contexts which bear a strong personal impression of the author. Yet is it possible to describe these word choices as statistically unusual against general patterns of word choice with any degree of precision? Must the study of word choice remain impressionistic?

There are, then, two basic problems in the analysis of individual styles of writing: one is that the elements of style may be too general to be privately characterizing – e.g. Orwell's military-pedantic style for Big Brother. The other is that some of the elements of style may not be general enough. That is, it is difficult to recognize absolute deviations in word choice and rhetorical presentation (not to mention content choice) in any piece of writing, since the systems from which the author may deviate cannot be described for any language as a whole, in any form that will meet scientific standards of explicitness.

Writing on 'The Semantics of Style', Chatman deals with the first of these difficulties:

> It should be noted . . . that taking style as individual manner does not require us to insist upon the uniqueness of each of its components. The fact that a feature charac-

teristic of an author's style was generally popular in his period or school does not make it any less characterizing of him. It is added to other features to make up his unique pattern or configuration. Because of its complex nature, the recognition of a writer's style is not a mere act of perception, as that term is generally defined, (for example, 'whenever we "perceive" what we name "a chair", we are interpreting a certain group of data [modification of the sense organs], and treating them as signs of a referent.') Perception entails the recognition of a thing as an instance of a CLASS of things, whereas style-recognition, as the recognition of a personality, is something more, namely the recognition of an individual as a unique complex or pattern of perceived features. That is why perception tends to be virtually instantaneous whereas the ability to recognize an author's style takes time to acquire.[12]

It seems as if Chatman is here defending the use of general components in determining the components of a stylistic perception, while suggesting that there are other components that take longer to interpret, perhaps specifically private ones, special to the individual perceived. Chatman may be right in his defence of an author's use of general components in a personalizing way. Although there are only a few 'optional' transformations, about a dozen or so at last count, they may be combined or employed in an unlimited number of ways to provide many different paraphrases, and if indeed the preference for one set of transformations over another is a sign of personality, there are certainly enough possibilities in the realm of syntax to fit anyone. By combination, anyone may sew himself together a syntactic suit of clothes that expresses his individuality.

This would be possible even if the basic components of the game were more abstract and limited than they seem to be. What could be more constricting than the rules of chess?

Yet how powerful is the sense of personality rising up from the games of Alekhine, Capablanca, Rubinstein, and dozens of others. Alekhine himself noticed this. In a remarkable passage from his work *My Best Games of Chess 1908–1923*, he isolates a feature highly characteristic of his own style, and yet it is derived from no element more personal than the rule defining the Bishop's move:

> The reader will clearly perceive a similarity with other games (which also gained brilliancy prizes) [Alekhine is here analyzing such a game, with Bogolojuboff in 1921] . . . The leading characteristic in these games is an unforeseen but immediately decisive attack.
>
> The chief point in these attacks lie in the fact that none of them was prepared in the immediate vicinity of its objective. On the contrary, all the preliminary manoeuvres which tended to divert the adverse pieces from the defense of their King took place in the centre or on the opposite wing. Furthermore, it is interesting to note that the deciding move, a real hammer-blow, is played by a Bishop and always involves sacrificial variations.
>
> These repeated attacks in the same manner, in the course of games of widely different character, seem to me to constitute a very precise criterion of a player's style.[13]

As Alekhine makes clear, the elements of personality in chess style are not different from those that make up its rules but are characteristic methods of applying and combining those general elements described in the rules. One component of the system of chess is rigorously and negatively determined: if a Bishop moves on a rank, it is not a move in chess. The other component is completely free – the strategy of the player. Indeed, the player is not even constrained to win; he may play brilliantly to lose, or to draw, or to stalemate – an analogue of the literary artist writing to be personally impersonal, or to construct a 'person' from a collage of impersonal materials. The potentialities for combination in language are much richer than those of chess in this regard. They even allow a certain degree of individuality to the hack who has made himself the voice of his time so successfully that he is indistinguishable from dozens of his fellows. This last is an individuality of sorts, but a poor one – where is the honour in being described as the perfect hack?

The opposing problem – that of the inherent non-generality of certain elements of language – is not so amenable to analysis as the problem of excessive generality. It could be said that while the determining of *general* patterns of word choice (general lexis) is a chimera for any language, *individual* lexis is usually well-defined – each person can produce statements that he himself will agree with, statements that, in theory, represent adequately the state of his lexis at any one time, and can exhaust the contents of his opinions on the world of facts at any one time. If, then, only individual lexis is capable of definition, it stands as the only viable criterion against which to judge the lexical choices of others. Perhaps all judgements of lexical deviation as a measure of style are really disguised personal judgements on the part of the critic, disguised from himself perhaps by a belief that he is speaking in the name of the English language (or any other language).

Riffaterre deals with just this dilemma. He postulates that the reader, who has been unconsciously characterizing the writer's private choice of words during the act of reading, is able intuitively to recognize a sudden deviancy in that choice of words. But this 'intuitive grasp' of the artist's style may well also be based on the reader's personal stylistic tendencies. In the field of lexical choice, all that a critic can do is declare modestly that the impression of personality based on lexis is derived from a personal judgement on his, the reader's, part. If the reader and the writer have certain language elements (syntax and phonology) fundamentally in common, meaningful statements can be made about deviation from general norms in these areas alone. Beyond that all is faith, and testimony of witness.

However, personal and impersonal elements may be divided in the search for personality. Human communication, properly so called, seems to be impossible without at least the potentiality of individual style, however defined. A tree or a sunset does not have a 'style'; it would sound very odd to say that it did. It is true that the word 'communication' is sometimes used by information theorists to signify any emission and reception of information, but this would make 'communication' possible between a man and a sunset, and this in a non-metaphorical sense; after all, the man receives information from the sunset, and he assumes that nothing but the sunset emits the information. The ordinary use of the word 'communication' implies an *intention* to contact, and intention can be postulated only for human beings. A dog's 'intention' to communicate is, I think, an act of anthropomorphizing, and the Being that emits information from the light of setting suns is, despite Wordsworth, a hypothesis.

The emitter of information must be recognized as human for intention to be imputed, and therefore for a communication to be truly communicative. There must, in other words, be the potentiality in the signal as received and interpreted for the message to have had a different form; there must be a base identificative component and a non-base stylistic component for communication to take place.

However, this is only to say that the penultimate grade of stylistic perception operates enough to identify the emitter of information as human. Why is there an ultimate stage of apprehension, that of individual personality? Why is the style the man? Perhaps human beings need to defend themselves against a ceaseless necessity to generalize caused by an excess of sensory information. There is always present in the process of interpreting the millions of physical alterations in the sense-organs produced by the physical universe a tendency to see the whole universe as one huge 'ditto' sign, a sign which suppresses novelty in the name of sanity. Literature has been described by a number of modern critics as an opposing force to these deadly acts of generalization, an assertion of individual freedom and personal coherence. Father Walter Ong finds that

> all verbalization, including all literature, is radically a cry, a sound emitted from the interior of a person, a modification of one's exhalation of breath which retains the intimate connection with life which we find in breath itself. [With this modified exhalation] persons commune with persons, reaching one another's interiors in a way which one can never reach the interior of an 'object'.

The function of language is intimately associated with this 'interiority':

> Language retains this interiority because it, and the concepts that are born with it, remain always the medium wherein persons discover and renew their discovery that they are persons, that is, discover and renew their own proper interiority and selves.[14]

Other critics, like Georges Poulet, find in the exposure of interiority less a passive appreciation of another's 'exhalations', like Father Ong, and more an active attack on the integral self of the reader or listener:

> Because of the strange invasion of my person by the thoughts of another, I am a self who is granted the experience of thinking thoughts foreign to me . . . Reading is just that: a way of giving way not only to a host of alien words, images, ideas, but also to the very alien principle which utters them and shelters them . . . Reading implies something resembling the apperception I have of my self, the action by which I grasp straightway what I think as being thought by a subject (who, in this case, is not I).[15]

The description of the characteristics of the alien object in terms of the linguistic structures it contains, that is, those clues to performance that assist the subjective consciousness to identify it as Other, is the subtlest task of modern stylistics. Certainly, if Father Ong is right, the 'voice' in literature bears the most intimate signs of its origin in the personality of another. And as students of language we must be prepared to say from what elements, precisely, this image of 'another' is derived, if this description is possible.

We must not assume that all human artefacts and pursuits are inherently describable by human beings, simply because human beings produce and enjoy them. It has been seriously suggested that the ultimate reaches of music and chess are beyond the power of human description and will remain so. Perhaps the same is true of literature. What a study of style based upon language can undertake, therefore, is essentially a 'silhouetting' function: a linguistic stylistics can distinguish those elements of a literary work that attain their effect from public norms and operate to mime the world of facts and processes, and can also distinguish public components of a subjectivity which is felt by the reader to form part of another personality. The limit may be reached when the alien personality expresses itself only as itself. Before the ultimate expression of privacy the public voice falls silent.

5 CONCLUDING COMMENTS

IN the previous pages we have seen two games being played, a public and a private one. In the public literature game the facts of language are mobilized to mime anything in the universe *except* the private depths of the speaker. In the private game, the facts of language are mobilized to mime nothing in the universe *but*, ultimately, the private depths of the speaker.

The public game is played (by the Greek rules) out of belief that private depths are ineffable and, at any rate, of less importance than social roles. In its purest form, Aristotle's criticism, there is the implicit belief that the personal idiosyncrasies of a great creator will reveal the bare rules of the game he is playing, and are to be imitated by all those who wish to play the game after him. The creator employing the facts of language in a public language game played between him and his readers or hearers, reveals everything but himself. The only 'self' that emerges is the public self of a game player. However, since this game is the noblest game of all, that of revealing the binding significances of human life, the role of game player is not a trivial one.

This desire to reveal all else but the ineffable (and

perhaps trivial) depths of the personality is not the modern game. The modern, private game, played by the Romans first, and later by the Romantics and Post-Romantics, uses even the most objective rules in an attempt to portray the artist. Joyce, the modern master of this branch of the literary game, and Mahler, the modern master in this advanced stage of the musical game, have drawn portraits of themselves as system collectors; their materials are the systems of others. Has Joyce written novels, or 'novels'? Has Mahler written symphonies, or 'symphonies'? This development is the final form of the Romantic attempt to portray the individual, a development in a paradoxical but logical direction.

In playing both of these stylistic games, however, human beings are constantly reforming and transforming the world, inner and outer. In the long run, the *what* is created by the *how*. The results of this process are literature and society. Whether the world is grateful for having been 'produced' we will probably never know, but human beings cannot endure not producing the world. A juggler, using immense skill to construct a wheel of objects in the air, is an image of the human being at his typical work; if the skill or will, the *how* falters, the *what* disintegrates, and chaos is immediate and irretrievable. By sustaining the world, through public and private games of style, the human being forms a subsistent reality, a standing-wave of being.

NOTES

1 Style as perceptive strategy

1 Huxley, A., *Point Counter Point*, orig. pub. 1928, Perennial Classic ed. (New York: Harper & Row, 1965), pp. 32–3, 34–5.
2 Weltner, K., *The Measurement of Verbal Information in Psychology and Education*, trans. B. M. Crook (Berlin, Heidelberg and New York: Springer-Verlag, 1973), pp. 103–7.
3 Chatman, S., 'The Semantics of Style', in Kristeva, J., *et al.* (eds), *Essays in Semiotics* (*Approaches to Semiotics* 4, ed. T. Sebeok) (The Hague: Mouton, 1971), pp. 399–422.

2 Types of linguistic criticism

1 Vygotsky, L., 'Thought and Speech' (from Chapter VII of *Language and Thought*), quoted in Saporta, S. (ed.), *Psycholinguistics: a Book of Readings* (New York: Holt, Rinehart and Winston, 1961), p. 576.
2 For a description of 'casual' and 'non-casual' discourse, see Voegelin, C. F., 'Casual and Noncasual Utterances within Unified Structure', in Sebeok, T. (ed.), *Style in Language* (Cambridge, Mass.: MIT Press, 1960), pp. 57–68.
3 The main treatments of this notion are Austin, J., *How to Do Things with Words* (London: Oxford University Press, 1962), and Searle, J., *Speech Acts: an Essay in the Philosophy of Language* (Cambridge: Cambridge University Press, 1969).
4 Searle, J., op. cit., p. 66.
5 Ohmann, R., 'Speech Acts and the Definition of Literature', *Philosophy and Rhetoric*, IV (1971), pp. 1–19.

6 For a discussion of illocutionary forms in Blake's *Tyger*, see Epstein, E. L., 'The Self-Reflexive Artefact: an Approach to a Theory of Value in Literature', in Fowler, R. (ed.), *Style and Structure in Literature: Essays in the New Stylistics* (Ithaca, NY: Cornell University Press and Oxford: Basil Blackwell, 1975), pp. 40–78.

7 Vygotsky, L., op. cit., p. 535.

8 Quoted in Slobin, D. I., *Psycholinguistics* (Glenview, Ill. and London: Scott, Foresman, 1971), p. 101.

9 Ohmann, R., 'Generative Grammars and the Concept of Literary Style', *Word*, XX (1964), pp. 424–39. Ohmann's analysis is basically transformational-generative (Chomskyan); for a description of Chomskyan principles of syntactic analysis, see Fowler, R., *Linguistics and the Novel* (London: Methuen, 1977), pp. 6 ff.

3 Playing the literature game – a public and collective norm

1 Lieberman, P., *Intonation, Perception, and Language* (Cambridge, Mass.: MIT Press, 1967), p. 125. See also Cairns, H. S., and Cairns, C. C., *Psycholinguistics: A Cognitive View of Language* (New York: Holt, Rinehart and Winston, 1976), pp. 120–44, for a treatment of the interpretive process in phonology.

2 Lieberman, P., op. cit., pp. 165–6.

3 Joos, M., *The Five Clocks: a Linguistic Excursion Into the Five Styles of English Usage* (New York: Harcourt, Brace and World, 1967, orig. pub. 1962), p. 37.

4 Letter to Henry Cromwell, 25 November 1710. (Pope tried to give the impression that he had written much the same letter to William Walsh on 22 October 1706; see Sherburn, G. (ed.), *The Correspondence of Alexander Pope*, I (Oxford: The Clarendon Press, 1956), pp. 105–8).

For commentary on the Ajax lines, see (among many others), Tillotson, G., *On the Pastoral Poetry of Pope* (London: Oxford University Press, 1938), pp. 124–30, 150–1; Fussell, P., *Poetic Meter and Poetic Form* (New York: Random House, 1965), p. 43 (where he notices the lack of dissimilation of the sibilants in the first Ajax line, but not the lack of dissimilation of the 't's); and S. Chatman's treatment of these lines in *A Theory of Meter* (The Hague: Mouton, 1965). Lotspeich, C. M., 'The Metrical Technique of Pope's Illustrative Couplets', *JEGP*, 26 (1927), pp. 471–4, while short and not detailed in treatment,

makes the point that Pope forces the reader to read the lines by
manipulating his sense of the language. See also Adler, J. H.,
'Pope and the Rules of Prosody', *PMLA*, 76 (1961), pp. 218–26.

5 See Lieberman, P., op. cit., pp. 144 ff. For sensitive treatments
of intonation from slightly different viewpoints, see Bolinger,
D., *Aspects of Language*, 2nd ed. (New York: Harcourt Brace
Jovanovich, 1975), pp. 48–52 and *passim*; Lehiste, I., *Supraseg-
mentals* (Cambridge, Mass.: MIT Press, 1970); Palmer, F. R.
(ed.), *Prosodic Analysis* (London: Oxford University Press,
1969); Crystal, D., *Prosodic Systems and Intonation in English*
(Cambridge: Cambridge University Press, 1969).

6 See Chomsky, N., and Halle, M., *The Sound Pattern of English*
(New York: Harper & Row, 1968), for a treatment of stress-
pattern in English words and phrases. See also Schmerling,
S. F., *Aspects of English Sentence Stress* (Austin, Tex. and London:
University of Texas Press, 1976) and Catford, J. C., *Funda-
mental Problems in Phonetics* (Bloomington, Ind. and London:
University of Indiana Press, 1977).

7 Lieberman, P., op. cit., p. 145.

8 Ladefoged, P., in *A Course in Phonetics* (New York: Harcourt
Brace Jovanovich, 1975), pp. 97–102, supports the traditional
view of a two-stress system for English. See, however, Epstein,
E. L., and Hawkes, T., *Linguistics and English Prosody* (University of Buffalo, Studies in Linguistics, 1958).

9 Nabokov, V., *Notes on Prosody* (New York: Pantheon Books,
Bollingen Series 72a, 1964), pp. 9–17.

10 For 'paralinguistics', see Crystal, D., op. cit.

11 Chomsky, N., *Syntactic Structures* (The Hague: Mouton, 1957),
pp. 35–6.

12 Jespersen, O., *A Modern English Grammar on Historical Principles* (Copenhagen: Ejnar Munksgaard, 1927), Vol. II, 17.1–
17.3.

13 Lowell, R., *Salem*, from *Lord Weary's Castle and the Mills of the
Kavanaughs* (New York: Harcourt, Brace and World, 1961,
orig. pub. 1944), p. 32.

14 See Bolinger, D., 'Linear Modification', *PMLA*, 67 (1952),
pp. 1117–44; and 'Adjectives in English: Attribution and
Predication', *Lingua*, 18 (1967), pp. 1–34.

15 Epstein, E. L., 'Hopkins' *Heaven-Haven*: A Linguistic–Critical
Description', *Essays in Criticism*, 23 (April 1973), pp. 137–45;
Epstein, E. L., in Fowler, R., op. cit.; Epstein, E. L., 'Blake's
Infant Sorrow – an Essay in Discourse Analysis', in Kachru,
B., and Stahlke, H. (eds), *Current Trends in Stylistics* (Papers in

84 LANGUAGE AND STYLE

Linguistics Monographs, Linguistic Research Incorporated, Edmonton, Alberta, Canada, 1972), pp. 231–41; Halliday, M. A. K., 'The Linguistic Study of Literary Texts', in Lunt, H. G. (ed.), *Proceedings of the Ninth International Congress in Linguistics* (The Hague: Mouton, 1964), pp. 302–7; Epstein, E. L., 'Yeats' Experiments with Syntax in the Treatment of Time', in Porter, R., and Brophy, J. (eds), *Modern Irish Literature: A William York Tindall Festschrift* (New Rochelle, New York: Iona College Press/Twayne Publishers, 1972), pp. 171–84; Epstein, E. L., 'Detemporalized Syntax in the Poetry of Yeats', in *Style and Text: a Nils Erik Enkvist Festschrift* (Stockholm, Sweden: Språkförlaget Skriptor, 1975), pp. 305–16; Perloff, M., *The Poetic Art of Robert Lowell* (Ithaca, NY: Cornell University Press, 1973); Freeman, D. C., 'Syntax and Poetics in Three Odes of John Keats' (forthcoming); Freeman, D. C., 'The Strategy of Fusion: Dylan Thomas's Syntax', in Fowler, R., op. cit; Chatman, S., 'Milton's Participal Style', *PMLA*, 83 (1968), pp. 1386–99; Fairley, I., 'Syntactic Deviation and Cohesion', *Language and Style*, 6 (1973), pp. 216–29; Fairley, I., *E. E. Cummings and Ungrammar; A Study of Syntactic Deviance in his Poems* (New York: Watermill Publishers, 1975); Keyser, S. J., 'Towards a Theory of Poetic Form and Meaning', *College English;* (forthcoming); Fish, S., 'Literature in the Reader: Affective Stylistics', *New Literary History*, 2 (Autumn 1970), pp. 123–62; Fish, S., *Surprised by Sin: The Reader in Paradise Lost* (Berkeley, Calif.: University of California Press, 1971); Fish, S., *Self-Consuming Artifacts* (Berkeley, Calif.: University of California Press, 1972).

See also Baker, W. E., *Syntax in English Poetry 1870–1930* (Berkeley, Calif.: University of California Press, 1967). Donald Davie's seminal work *Articulate Energy* (London: Routledge, 1955) provided much of the early impetus for the study of syntax in literature.

Roman Jakobson's contributions to this field, as to all fields of the study of the language of literature, has been enormous, and the mere listing of his articles and notes on the subject would amount to a listing of a fair portion of his *Collected Works* (for a bibliography, see Janua Linguarum series minor, no. 134, The Hague: Mouton, 1971). For an incisive commentary on Jakobson's principles of analysis, see Culler, J., *Structuralist Poetics: Structuralism, Linguistics, and the Study of Literature* (Ithaca, NY: Cornell University Press, 1975), pp. 55–74.

4 The private game: portraits of the artist

1 Spitzer, L., *Linguistics and Literary History: Essays in Stylistics* (Princeton, NJ: Princeton University Press, 1948). See also his two volumes of *Stilstudien* (Munich: Hueber, 1961). Other important works in the same critical field of Romantic Individualist analysis are Vossler, K., *Frankreichs Kultur im Spiegel seiner Sprachentwicklung* (Heidelberg: Carl Winter, 1913); and his *Gesammelte Aufsatze zur Sprachphilosophie* (Munich: Hueber, 1923).

2 Burgess, A., *Joysprick* (London and New York: André Deutsch, Harcourt Brace Jovanovich, 1973), pp. 62–81. The entire book is impressive, but see also the chapter on 'Borrowed Styles', pp. 93–109.

3 For a suggestive treatment of the idea that the concept of the *mot juste* necessarily involves the death of individual style, see Purdy, S., 'Henry James, Gustave Flaubert, and the Ideal Style', *Language and Style*, 3 (1970), pp. 163–84.

4 *Ulysses* (New York: Random House edition, reset 1961), p. 51.

5 Milic, Louis T., *A Quantitative Approach to the Style of Jonathan Swift* (The Hague: Mouton, 1967). Kiparsky, P., 'The Role of Linguistics in a Theory of Poetry', *Daedalus*, 102, 3 (1973), pp. 221–44; he also discusses some of the patterning to be found in the poetry of Dylan Thomas. Ohmann, R., 'Prolegomena to the Analysis of Prose Style', in Martin, H. C. (ed.), *Style in Prose Fiction* (New York: Columbia University Press, 1959); Ohmann, R., *Shaw: the Style and the Man* (Middletown, Connecticut: Wesleyan University Press, 1962); Ohmann, R., 'Generative Grammars and the Concept of Literary Style', *Word*, 20 (1964), pp. 423–39 (on the style of Hemingway, Faulkner, Lawrence and James); Ohmann, R., 'Literature as Sentences', *College English*, 27 (1966), pp. 261–7; Ohmann, R., 'A Linguistic Appraisal of Victorian Style', in Levine, G., and Madden, W. (eds), *The Art of Victorian Prose* (New York and London: Oxford University Press, 1968) (on the style of Matthew Arnold); see also Chatman, S., *The Later Style of Henry James* (Oxford: Blackwells, 1972).

Ohmann's essay 'Mentalism in the Study of Literary Language', in Zale, E. M. (ed.), *Proceedings of the Conference on Language and Language Behavior* (New York: Appleton-Century-Crofts, 1968), pp. 188–212, is the source of the statement that 'literary criticism is the study of mental structures' (p. 210).

In this important essay, Ohmann argues that there is a competence in creativity comparable to the 'linguistic competence' by which the ordinary speaker constructs and understands the sentences of his language. In the course of the essay Ohmann deals with the linguistic choices made (probably outside of awareness) by Gibbon, Saul Bellow, Henry James, Yeats, Keats, and Richard Wilbur, and finds in them signs of the separate individuality of these writers.

For a statistical approach to the analysis of style, see Doležel, L., and Bailey, R. W. (eds), *Statistics and Style* (New York, London and Amsterdam: Elsevier, 1969).

For a sensitive treatment of the theoretical issues involved in deciding whether style is an individualizing factor or composed of general linguistic elements, see Hirsch, E. D., 'Stylistics and Synonymity', *Critical Inquiry*, 1 (1975), pp. 559–79. Langbaum, R., *The Mysteries of Identity* (New York: Oxford University Press, 1977).

6 Ohmann, R., *Shaw: the Style and the Man*, pp. xi–xiii.

7 Ohmann, R., 'Generative Grammar and the Concept of Literary Style'.

8 Orwell, G., *1984* (New York: Signet, 1961, orig. pub. 1949), p. 42.

9 One attempt to arrive at general descriptions of deviations from a general norm was made by P. Guiraud, in *Les Caractères Statistiques du Vocabulaire* (Paris: Presses Universitaires de France, 1954). For treatments of the problems inherent in the study of style by statistical methods, see Bailey, R. W., 'Statistics and Style: a Historical Survey', in Doležel, L., and Bailey, R. W. (eds), *Statistics and Style*, pp. 217–36.

10 The data on Joyce and Yeats are derived from Hanley, M., *Word Index to James Joyce's Ulysses* (Madison, Wis.: University of Wisconsin Press, 1951, orig. pub. 1937), and Parrish, S. M. (ed.), *A Concordance to the Poems of William Butler Yeats* (Ithaca, NY: Cornell University Press, 1963). The material from the *Wake* derived from Hart, C., *A Concordance to Finnegans Wake* (Minneapolis, Minn.: University of Minnesota Press, 1963).

11 Riffaterre, M., 'Criteria for Style Analysis', *Word*, 15 (1959), pp. 154–74; 'Stylistic Context', *Word*, 16 (1960), pp. 207–18; 'Problèmes d'Analyse du Style Littéraire', *Romance Philology*, 14 (1961), pp. 216–27; 'Vers la Définition du "Style"', *Word*, 17 (1961), pp. 318–44; 'The Stylistic Function', in Lunt, H. (ed.), *Proceedings of the Ninth International Congress of Linguists* (The Hague: Mouton, 1964).

12 Chatman, S., in Kristera *et al.* (eds), pp. 417–18. See p. 81.

13 Alekhine, London, 1957, p. 138.

14 Ong, W. J. (S.J.), 'A Dialectic of Aural and Objective Correlatives', *Essays in Criticism*, 8 (1958), pp. 73–108.

15 Poulet, G., 'The Phenomenology of Reading', *New Literary History*, I, 1 (October 1969), pp. 53–68.

BIBLIOGRAPHICAL NOTE

The literature of stylistics is enormous and extremely diffuse in focus. The two aspects of the meaning of the word 'style' treated in the text above represent two emphases or directions of study, and the influence of these emphases is to be felt in many studies, in more or less palpable form. However, the literature includes articles and books in old-fashioned literary criticism, old-fashioned philosophical and psychological criticism, and, indeed, in every sort of criticism, old- or new-fashioned, and in every conceivable field. This note is, therefore, highly selective. For an article which sums up the diverse trends in stylistics in a short compass, consult Freeman, D. C., 'Linguistics and the Study of Literature: Ends and Beginnings', in Brown, H. D., and Wardhaugh, R. (eds), *A Survey of Applied Linguistics* (Ann Arbor, Michigan: University of Michigan Press, (forthcoming). An earlier treatment of the diversity of the field is Hough, G., *Style and Stylistics* (London: Routledge & Kegan Paul, 1969). In both of these references there are useful bibliographical guides. This is also true of Enkvist, N. E., *Linguistic Stylistics* (The Hague: Mouton, 1973).

There are two general bibliographies of stylistic studies in English: Milic, L. T., *Style and Stylistics: an Analytical Bibliography* (New York: The Free Press, 1967); Bailey, R. W., and Burton, D., SND, *English Stylistics: a Bibliography* (Cambridge, Mass.: MIT Press, 1968).

The basic bibliography for studies in Romance stylistics is Hatzfeld, H., *A Critical Bibliography of the New Stylistics, Applied to the Romance Literatures, 1900–52* (Chapel Hill, NC: North Carolina

Studies in Comparative Literature, 5, 1953). For later work in Romance stylistics, see Hatzfeld, H., and Le Hir, Y., *Essai de Bibliographie Critique de Stylistic Française et Romane, 1955–1960* (Paris: Presses Universitaires de France, 1961). Todorov, T., 'Les Etudes du Style: Bibliographie Sélective', *Poétique*, 2 (1970), pp. 224–32, is also to be consulted. See also the 'Selective Bibliography' by Martin, H. C., and Ohmann, R. in Candelaria, F. (ed.), *Perspectives on Style* (Boston: Allyn and Bacon, 1968).

There are a number of journals in the field, of which *Language and Style: an International Journal*, *Style*, and *Lingua e Stile* are devoted specifically to the topics of linguistic stylistics. (*Style* publishes a continuing series of bibliographical articles.) The Annual Bibliography of the Modern Language Association has a section devoted to stylistics. Other continuing bibliographies are to be found in the *Bibliographie Linguistique*, the *Year's Work in English Studies*, the *Year's Work in Modern Language Studies*, and *Language and Language Behavior Abstracts*.

There are a number of collections of essays in stylistics which collectively give a good picture of the range of techniques available to the student of linguistics and literature. Sebeok, T. A. (ed.), *Style in Language* (Cambridge, Mass.: MIT Press, 1960), contains a number of interesting articles, including Jakobson's seminal statement on the poetic function of language – the concentration by the hearer/reader on the 'code' of the message in its own terms. The essay by C. F. Voegelin makes the useful distinction between 'casual' and 'non-casual' speech situations, with literary situations being 'non-casual'. Other useful anthologies in the field are Chatman, S., and Levin, S. R. (eds), *Essays in the Language of Literature* (Boston: Houghton, Mifflin, 1967), and Love, G. A., and Payne, M. (eds), *Contemporary Essays on Style* (Chicago: University of Chicago Press, 1969). See especially the essays by Riffaterre and Milic (in Chatman and Levin) on criteria for style analysis, and on the problems involved in making a typology of styles.

The most up to date and, in some ways, the widest ranging of the anthologies is Freeman, D. C. (ed.), *Linguistics and Literary Style*, (New York: Holt, Rinehart and Winston, 1970). Especially useful is the section on the method of linguistic analysis of literary artefacts, containing theoretical and practical descriptions of specific methods of analysis. A more traditional collection is Cunningham, J. V., *The Problem of Style* (New York: Fawcett Books, 1966), which contains generally short selections from a wide range of contributors, only a few of whom can be termed linguists. Other anthologies include Chatman, S. (ed.), *Literary Style: a Symposium*

90 LANGUAGE AND STYLE

(London and New York: Oxford University Press, 1971), Fowler, R., *Style and Structure in Literature: Essays in the New Stylistics* (Oxford: Basil Blackwell, 1975), and Ringbom, H. (ed.), *Style and Text: Studies presented to Nils Erik Enkvist* (Stockholm: Språkförlaget Skriptor, 1975). A small volume containing essays from a meeting of the English Institute edited by S. Chatman (*Approaches to Poetics*, New York: Columbia University Press, 1973) contains six essays of considerable interest, by V. Erlich, H. Davidson, F. Kermode, R. Ohmann, S. Fish and T. Todorov, on the systems of Jakobson and Barthes and on stylistic methodology in general. Fish's article asks the important question, 'What is stylistics and why are they saying such terrible things about it?' and answers it with a close examination of some prevalent assumptions made by stylisticians.

Some other, rather more specialized, anthologies are Levine, G., and Madden, W. (eds), *The Art of Victorian Prose* (New York: Oxford University Press, 1968), and Doležel, L., and Bailey, R. W. (eds), *Statistics and Style* (New York, London and Amsterdam: Elsevier, 1969). (See also their *Annotated Bibliography of Statistical Stylistics*, in the Michigan Slavic Series, Ann Arbor, Mich.: University of Michigan Press, 1968.)

The materials and bibliographical listings in the above works and in those additional works mentioned in the footnotes to this book can provide an interested student with an entry into a field of enormous interest and complexity.

INDEX